THE FINAL YEARS OF THOMAS HARDY, 1912-1928

The Final Years of
Thomas Hardy,
1912–1928

HAROLD OREL

First published 1976 by
THE MACMILLAN PRESS LTD
London and Basingstoke
Associated companies in New York
Dublin Melbourne Johannesburg and Madras

SBN 333 19454 3

Printed in Great Britain by
WESTERN PRINTING SERVICES LTD
Bristol

To Sara and Tim

Contents

List of Plates

Between pages 56–57

1 Thomas Hardy, a sketch by William Rothenstein, 1915

2a Emma Lavinia Hardy in her later years

2b Hardy at the turn of the century

3a Max Gate when first built, showing Conquer Barrow

3b The garden at Max Gate

4a Cartoon by H. Furness, 1923

4b Bust by Hamo Thorneycroft

5a With Gwen Ffrangcon-Davies ('Tess')

5b Poster for the Kingsway Theatre production of *The Dynasts*

6 Hardy and Florence on their way to vote

7 With Edmund Gosse at Max Gate, 1927

8 The Prince of Wales' visit, 1923

The above are reproduced by permission of the following: no. 1, in the Spencer Library, University of Kansas, Sir John and Mr Michael Rothenstein; no. 4a, National Portrait Gallery; no. 8, Mr James and Mr Gregory Stevens-Cox; remainder, Dorset County Museum.

Acknowledgements

I wish to thank the world-wide community of scholars who have done so much to evaluate wisely the nature and quality of Thomas Hardy's literary achievements. On their scholarship and insights much of this study has been based. Four men in particular have encouraged me, because they share my conviction that a new look at the final phase of Hardy's life is justified: Professor J. O. Bailey, recently retired from the University of North Carolina; Professor Walter Wright of the University of Nebraska; Professor Dale Kramer of the University of Illinois; and Professor Mamoru Osawa of the Kanazawa College of Fine Arts in Japan. Their distinguished writings on Hardy will be read by many future generations of students interested in Hardy's development as an artist.

Needed time for the study was made possible, in generous measure, by a grant awarded by the National Endowment for the Humanities, and by additional aid received from the General Research Fund of the University of Kansas. I am grateful to the Thomas Hardy Society for permission to reprint Chapter 8, with some revisions, from *Thomas Hardy and the Modern World*, edited by F. B. Pinion and published by the Society in 1974.

Finally, I would like to acknowledge the help and wisdom of a colleague and friend of some two decades now, George J. Worth. He, too, is a friend of Thomas Hardy.

August 1975   H.O.

Introduction

The dangers of superimposing a consistent philosophy on Thomas Hardy's widely disparate poems are fully as great as Hardy, in his preface to *Poems of the Past and the Present*, claimed they were:

> ... that portion which may be regarded as individual comprises a series of feelings and fancies written down in widely differing moods and circumstances, and at various dates; it will probably be found, therefore, to possess little cohesion of thought or harmony of colouring. I do not greatly regret this. Unadjusted impressions have their value, and the road to a true philosophy of life seems to lie in humbly recording diverse readings of its phenomena as they are forced upon us by chance and change.

When, to this caveat, a conscientious reader adds his uneasy awareness of the problems created by Hardy's failure to date a large number of his poems, Hardy's willingness to use poems written during any of several decades for a new collection, Hardy's warning that the 'mere impressions of the moment' should not be mistaken for 'convictions or arguments', and Hardy's hope that 'finely-touched spirits' among his readers would be sufficiently alert for 'right note-catching', he may well conclude the poet has presented him with 'miscellanies of verse', with all the dilemmas of ordering and analysis that such miscellanies inevitably impose.

I do not intend to demonstrate the existence of a hitherto unsuspected order of lyrics or of a previously unimagined consistency of intention and mood. Hardy's denials are convincing enough to render suspect the efforts of a number of critics over the past quarter-century to identify and define 'poetic structure' of entire volumes of Hardy's verse. Moreover, my concern is not with Hardy's total poetic output, but with only five of the volumes published after the appearance of *The Dynasts, Part Third*, in 1908: *Satires of Circumstance, Lyrics and Reveries* in 1914, *Moments of Vision* in 1917, *Late Lyrics and Earlier* in 1922, *Human Shows* in 1925, and *Winter Words* in 1928, a period of approximately fifteen years. (Practically all the poems in *Time's Laughingstocks*, 1910, were written prior to, or concurrently with, the writing of *The Dynasts*.) Not all, but much of this poetry is the work of a writer who has renounced prose fiction as his primary medium of artistic expression, and it is possible to recognise – among those poems which are topical, datable, and identifiably the work of a poet writing in his seventh decade and beyond – not only groupings of poems, with distinct categories of subject-matter, but a texture of attitudes. Some of them were much more sombre and cheerless than perhaps even Hardy's contemporaries appreciated, and became increasingly so toward the end.

Nor should these observations surprise us. Even if Hardy's opinions on many major concerns were as firmly established by the mid-1860s as has often been alleged, a mature artist will express himself differently from a callow youth; we do not have anywhere near as much information as we would like on a number of crucial periods and relationships in Hardy's life; history has a way of changing focus and redistributing emphases on matters that have long since seemed settled; and Hardy, no less than any Victorian poet (with the possible exception of Yeats), was continually rethinking his relationship to the past. If Hardy allowed too many poems to get into print, there exists no consensus as to which poems should have been prevented from seeing the light of day, and indeed all the poems tell us something we would not willingly do without. The poems – we know – were carefully ordered by Hardy; their arrangement was not haphazard, even if Hardy confessed, with some bafflement, that 'irrelation was almost unavoidable with efforts so diverse'. There is a *late* Hardy in the poetry, just as there is a distinguishable apprentice novelist in *Desperate Remedies*, *Under the Greenwood Tree*, and *A Pair of Blue Eyes*; there are phases of development in Hardy's poetic career; and even though the problem of distinguishing what is early and what is late is compounded by Hardy's peculiar habits of composition, revising, and publication, the effort is worth making.

When Hardy dictated to his second wife his autobiography (most of which employed the third person and gave to his life a somewhat ghostly remoteness), he anticipated the possibility that the work might appear in two volumes. Even though he did not complete the work – Mrs Hardy was largely responsible for the account of the years after 1918 – and the years with which we are most concerned in this study, i.e. 1912–28, are treated in the *Life* almost as sketchily as his own childhood, he added at the top of the first page of the 'rough copy' of the typescript of what was to become *The Later Years of Thomas Hardy*,[1] in his calligraphic hand, the words: 'Mem.:/Vol. II might begin here – if 2 vols.'

As a consequence, the biography splits into two volumes, *The Early Life of Thomas Hardy, 1840–1891*, ending with the publication of *Tess of the d'Urbervilles*, and *The Later Years of Thomas Hardy, 1892–1928*, beginning with the critical and popular reception of *Tess*.

Nevertheless, as Helmut E. Gerber and W. Eugene Davis have noted, 'The neat dichotomy suggested by the titles of Hardy's disguised auto-biography . . . should not be taken too seriously', not only for the reasons that these editors suggest – 'the tremendous quantity of *belles lettres* (almost entirely verse and drama)' that he wrote in his later years, and his ability to continue to see and experience life 'with unusual clarity'[2] – but for the fact that at least three years other than 1891 might be chosen to illustrate the moment when his life was dramatically redirected to new goals. For example, 1895 – the year in which *Jude the Obscure* was published – or 1896, the year in which Hardy's disgust at the hostile reception of *Jude* led to the diary entry of 17 October 1896, 'Perhaps I can express more fully in verse ideas and emotions which run counter to the inert crystallized opinion – hard as a rock – which the vast body of men have vested inter-ests in supporting.'[3] Or 1908, the year in which *The Dynasts, Part Third*, was printed, completing not only Hardy's longest poetical work (and one of the longest poems in English literature), but ending a lifelong obsession with the events, characters, and significance of the bloodiest years of the nineteenth century.

I have chosen 1912, however, as the moment with which to open a reconsideration of Thomas Hardy's final period. It was a year of profound significance to Hardy. Emma Lavinia's death reminded him how much, at one time, he had loved the maiden 'fair-eyed and white-shouldered, broad-browed and brown-tressed' whom he had met at the Cornish rectory of St Juliot. The trite metaphor of embers coming back to life, of how memories of lyrical love can fan flames, proved valid; for Hardy's 'Poems of 1912–13', published as part of a longer work – *Satires of Circum-stance, Lyrics and Reveries* (1914) – are fresher, more passionate, more deeply felt, than most of the love poems he had published up to this point. They were written by a poet who had already used up his three-score-and-ten. And they signalled the continuing right of a major poet to hold the attention of his audience: who could guess what else he might offer in the way of creative art before his course was run?

I should like, therefore, to begin the study with a review of the in-fluences that changed Hardy's childhood from an ordinary, obscure training for a countryman's existence to a series of opening doors that led to the larger world of London and of professional authorship. Hardy did not drift into success; he worked hard for it. He recognised and shrewdly evaluated opportunities as they arose – rejecting several as unsuitable to his needs and talents, but exploiting an astonishingly high number of those that were appropriate to self-advancement. Chapter 1 takes a closer look at the steps along the highway which Hardy travelled to become a citizen of Wessex and the world. Moreover, such a review of the factors that shaped his life suggests that Hardy never really retreated from a busy world into his own library, into his own mind. That mind was extraordinarily active, and well-informed on what was happening in the world. Social activities, of necessity, were slowing down; he made his last visit to London in 1920, and slept in a strange bed – away from his own at Max Gate – for the last time in 1923. But he met, saw, and corresponded with hundreds of people, and the notion (entertained by many residents of Dorchester) that Hardy was isolated either by his own wish or by his second wife's over-solicitous desire to spare his dwindling energies must be modified in the light of what we know about the constant stream of visitors to his home.

Primarily, however, this book studies the ways in which Hardy wrote about his continuing concerns in poetical form, and it attempts to use biographical information whenever possible to distinguish and define the boundary-lines between lyrical and dramatic expression.

The love poems dealing with the development, deterioration, and renewal of Hardy's tenderest feelings for Emma form a substantial fraction of the work we will be looking at. Perhaps Carl Weber's enthusiasm for the sequence, which led him to rank these poems after Elizabeth Barrett Browning's *Sonnets from the Portuguese* and Shakespeare's *Sonnets* – and ahead of Wordsworth's poems to Lucy, Matthew Arnold's poems to Marguerite, Rossetti's *House of Life*, and George Meredith's *Modern Love* – is excessive, but it is understandable; English literature, after all, has not specialised in a series of love poems recording genuine emotions rather than variations on courtly or literary conventions; and close examination of the merits of Hardy's poems may well lead to a final agreement with Weber's judgement (Chapter 2).

Because there has been some misunderstanding of Hardy's attitude toward the past, specifically the world of Dorset in the 1840s, I should like next to consider Hardy's poems about his childhood, customs observed when he was growing up (and when he presumably could enter into their observance with complete acceptance of their worth and trust in their permanence), and the people he knew then as grizzled elders, who were to become ghosts of Wessex (Chapter 3).

The occasional poems written to commemorate special moments of time contain many of Hardy's most eloquent and sage pronouncements on the human condition. There were more such poems, of a higher worth, than has generally been recognised (Chapter 4).

Hardy's appeal to readers all over the world – for example, in the Orient, where the Thomas Hardy Society of Japan is thriving – is in some measure predicated on an appreciation of his sincere feeling for natural landscape, expressed in many beautiful and striking poems. But Hardy, whose life was largely spent during the raging of the fierce debate over whether the forces of nature were benevolent or indifferent, or animated, in the words of Tennyson's *Maud*, in 'a world of plunder and prey', held no single or simple view about the relationship of the forces of nature to humanity. He was also deeply concerned with animals and birds; his compassion for the beasts of the field and the fowls of the air strengthened his friendship for Mrs Florence Henniker, and remained one of the few pleasures of the last two decades of his own marriage to Emma (Chapter 5).

The next chapter takes a long backward look at Hardy's interest in the theatre – a love affair of both the heart and mind that continued for more than six decades of his life, and shaped the unusual form of *The Dynasts*. *The Famous Tragedy of the Queen of Cornwall* was his final major effort as a creative artist, and in several respects has autobiographical resonances. An analysis of Hardy's concept of drama, which changed with time and became increasingly unconventional and determinedly anti-commercial, will define a significant element in his final years (Chapter 6).

Between 1912 and 1928 Hardy did not want to debate the question of the Immanent Will. That had long since been settled, and *The Dynasts,* his fullest statement, recapitulated views familiar not only to Hardy but to most serious thinkers in the second half of the nineteenth century. Rather, his concern was with the possible viability of the Christian religion in the modern age. In poem after poem he sought to demythologise Christian doctrine and liturgy. For example, his stand against miracles was a characteristically *reasoned* position. His views on Christianity are considered in Chapter 7.

Hardy had already recorded his views on war, at greater length, in *The Dynasts*; but the outbreak of the Great War, and its inevitable aftermath of disillusionment, of quarrelling and bitterness among former allies, convinced Hardy that still another cataclysm would take place. In some final poems – 'He Resolves to Say No More' probably being the last word Hardy wrote on the subject – he succumbed to a crushing, complete despair, and became at long last the pessimist he had always denied being (Chapter 8).

His ending was appropriate to the life he had lived, and more needs to be said about what he believed when that end came.

I
The Shaping of a Life

The portrait by William Strang, completed in 1893, that hangs in the National Portrait Gallery shows Hardy as a more sombre and thoughtful man – perhaps even sadder – than the young would-be dandy recorded in photographs of the 1860s. The grizzled Vandyke of 1892 had been trimmed back to a long, dark, drooping mustache. Tufts of hair curled over his ears. Strang caught Hardy – who at the time was completing *Jude the Obscure* – in a meditative moment, his balding head prominent, looking downward at something not within a viewer's line of vision.

Yet portraits made throughout his life show a man consistently wary, a man paying attention to the possibility that he might be sorry if he failed either to confront the photographer head-on or to watch him from a side-angle. This generalisation holds true of the Augustus John painting and the Youriévitch bust, both created very late in his life. About the latter, Hardy said, to Newman Flower, 'The Russian has put in that large curved nose without mercy.' The bust by Maggie Richardson (now at the Dorset County Museum, in the reconstructed Hardy study) replicates the watchful attitude in a most convincing fashion.

Why was his gaze so restless, dissatisfied? If one believes that toward the end he rested content in the knowledge that his poems captured moments of vision and made his readers aware of the nature of those visions – that he could do no more than 'notice such things', and remind his audience that they too should notice such things – and that this constituted sufficient triumph for an artist,[1] watchfulness becomes an appropriate and understandable element in his behaviour once he had passed his threescore-and-ten. He had 'hovering and "pouncing" eye-glances', said John Cowper Powys,[2] who met him at the close of his career.

But Hardy's alert, penetrating gaze upon the world antedated by many years his decision to become a professional writer. His 'intensity of regard', as Powys called it, had long been a notable aspect of his personality, and more than once his friends and acquaintances had discussed it. A problem of some important features of his early life should be reviewed.

First, there is the question of the kind of life Hardy, as the son of a master mason living on the very edge of Egdon Heath, might reasonably have been expected to lead as he came to manhood in the 1850s. He belonged to a family whose ancestors had been men and women of greater substance in Queen Elizabeth's reign, or in the time of William and Mary, than they were at any time in the eighteenth century. The decay of the d'Urberville fortunes may well be convincing as fiction because Hardy's attitude toward his own family heritage was tinged by regret mingled with bitterness. 'So we go down, down, down', he wrote when he described 'the decline and fall of the Hardys.'[3] Even though he knew that his father belonged to an independent class and could improve his social situation by exercising the energies of a Henchard, or even by luck, the possibility of a major elevation of class status remained unlikely if he followed in the steps of Thomas Hardy, his father. The paths that Hardy followed in order to escape the limitations imposed on the social caste of a bricklayer's family were, first, education; second, the career of an architect who travelled beyond the confines of Dorchester; and third, marriage. The end-result was something so close to detribalisation that guilt and remorse play very crucial roles in practically all the fictions that Hardy wrote after the mid-1870s.

Julia Augusta Martin, and not his mother, taught Hardy his letters. The fact has been widely known since the publication of five letters sent to the novelist from the mistress of the manor house of Kingston Maurward.[4] Nevertheless, its significance should be underscored: Hardy was singled out for this honour. Kingston Maurward was by far the handsomest estate in the neighbourhood, and 'the squire's wife', as Hardy was later to refer to her, took an intense personal interest in him even before she established a school in 1848 'for the education of children of the labouring classes'; Hardy learned his letters from her, fell in love with her, *then* attended her school for a year. She was more than the romantic 'lady of his dreams'; she served as an image of a higher class. Hardy, who recorded the fact of Francis Pitney Brouncker Martin's inability to retain the family fortune, who knew that Martin sold Kingston Maurward in 1853, and who learned from a variety of sources that 'the lady of his earliest passion as a child' had come down in the world (she wrote him on 21 April 1887 that she was now 'too poor' to buy a set of his works), must have reflected more than once on the ironies of changing social status. When Hardy transferred to a nonconformist day-school in Dorchester, his departure 'seriously wounded . . . this too sensitive lady'. Many years later, meditating on whether she or his mother (who had arranged the transfer) was more in the right, Hardy decided that perhaps Mrs Martin

had presumed too much, since his family were 'comparatively independent of the manor, as their house and the adjoining land were a family
lifehold, and the estate-work forming only part of Mr. Hardy's business.'[5]
Is it fanciful to see here Mrs Martin's patronising of an attractive, bright
child of lower class; her chagrin at being deprived of her star pupil;
and Mrs Hardy's resentment – however subdued in her son's tactfully
worded reminiscence – that she was considered ungrateful for not having
consulted Mrs Martin about the arrangements for young Tom's education?

Hardy's formal education consisted of the year at Mrs Martin's school,
followed by his studies at the Bockhampton school, his seven years at
Mr Last's Academy for Young Gentlemen, and his reading of Latin
('considered an extra'), French (taught him by a governess at his sister's
school), and German. Hardy describes himself as a 'born bookworm', and
there is no reason to doubt his studiousness; its consequences may be
seen in allusions to French and Latin classics scattered throughout his
later writings. The point, however, is that his was not the normal education shaped for utilitarian ends; he was not studying the 'practical'
subjects that the son of a mason, even the relatively well-off son of a
master mason, could easily put to use; nor was he being trained as a
countryman. Eight years of formal education altogether, then: Hardy
was to record in the *Life* 'that he had remained a child until he was sixteen', only to add, perhaps complacently, that nevertheless he had
'accomplished amazing things'. He had in mind what he had learned from
reading the classics and from studying the book of nature. In a subtle but
very real way, he had ordered a ticket for a destination different from any
reached by any member of all the earlier generations of Hardys. Distribution of credit must acknowledge Julia Augusta Martin and Isaac G.
Last as two crucial pedagogic influences; perhaps most of all Mrs Hardy,
who was, as her son wrote in an unsigned obituary in the *Dorset County
Chronicle* on 7 April 1904, 'a woman of strong character and marked
originality, with the keenest love for literature; and much of her son's
work in prose and verse was based upon her memories and opinions.'
For the *Daily Chronicle* (9 April) Hardy recalled that the first book
she had given him, 'after those merely for the nursery', was Dryden's
Virgil, 'for which she had a great liking', and he stated explicitly that
it was at her doing that his tutoring in Latin and French had taken
place.

The second stage in the process of self-definition and liberation from
mores that seemed increasingly provincial came not in the South Street
office of John Hicks, the Dorchester architect, but in the wider world of

London. Yet, before passing to the latter, we might note that the company he kept between 1856 and 1862 in the market-town he was later to
name Casterbridge had several unusual interests and aptitudes. John
Hicks himself competed with the young men working for him, testing
their knowledge of both Latin and Greek (Hardy was trying to learn how
to read the *Iliad*). William Barnes, the poet and schoolmaster, answered
difficult questions of grammar that neither Hardy nor Henry Bastow,
his fellow-pupil, could settle; Barnes, who taught next door to Hicks's
office, loomed increasingly large in Hardy's imagination, and his deep
faith in the value of native dialect in poems became an issue of some
concern to Hardy both as novelist and as poet of Dorset folkways; in
1879 Hardy, for the first and last time a reviewer, wrote high praise of
Barnes's *Poems of Rural Life in the Dorset Dialect*, and in 1886 he had the melancholy privilege of writing Barnes's obituary for the *Athenaeum*. Baptist-
bred Henry Bastow enlisted the aid of two enthusiastic, extraverted sons
of the Baptist minister of Dorchester, Frederick Perkins; the Greek
originals of scriptural passages bearing on the issue of adult baptism (and
many other lofty issues of small concern to the members of most architectural firms) were studied and quoted at length. And after Bastow,
whose four-year term ended so that an appointment to a London office
could begin (and later a Tasmanian one!), there came Hooper Tolbort,
one of the Reverend Barnes's pupils who was getting ready for a career in
the Indian Civil Service. In a lengthy obituary written for the *Dorset
County Chronicle* (16 August 1883), Hardy traced the steps of his 'remarkable' career, which culminated in the post of Deputy Commissioner of
Umballa before he died of consumption and was buried 'beside his
mother at the most beautiful spot in the Dorchester Cemetery, within
view of the hills and woods that his childhood knew well'. Hardy admired
Tolbort's 'marvellous passion for the acquisition of languages', which led
to the mastering of speaking and writing abilities in nine tongues; a
massive work, *The Portuguese in India*, for which Hardy tried (unsuccessfully)
to locate a publisher; and a scheme not unworthy of a grammarian with
Alexander's aspirations, 'for using Roman type for printing the verna-
culars of India and other Oriental tongues, so as to obviate the almost
insurmountable difficulty and expense of printing them in native
character'. High praise indeed: 'a sort of universalist in knowledge',
interested in photography, shorthand, chemistry, 'and what not', and 'a
supreme product of the great modern apparatus, competitive examination.'

   Tolbort was advised to present himself as a candidate at the Oxford
Middle-class Examination, 'where he took a first place among nine

hundred candidates', by Hardy's 'other' literary friend, Horace Moule, 'a fine Greek scholar . . . always ready to act the tutor in any classical difficulty', and possessed of a writing flair embodied in graceful reviews, leaders, and poems. Moule's influence on Hardy was exerted at critical moments: when Hardy asked for advice on whether he should continue reading Greek plays, Moule urged him to act prudently (Hardy might well have given up architecture in favour of a try at university studies if Moule had encouraged him); and again, in the early 1870s, when Hardy, dismayed by 'slating' reviews of his early fiction, wondered whether he should continue as a novelist, Moule urged him to persevere, partly on the pragmatic ground that fine architectural drawing might ruin his eyes, in which case literature would become 'a resource': Hardy could 'dictate a book, article, or poem, but not a geometrical design'.[6] Hardy may have overestimated his friend's poetical talents, but there is no question that the Hulsean prizeman of Queens' College, Cambridge, was an accomplished Greek scholar and musician; the brief tribute that Hardy wrote for a reprinting of his friend's poem 'Ave Caesar' in the *London Mercury* (October 1922) hardly begins to match the enormous respect that Hardy retained for more than half a century after Moule committed suicide in September 1873. (The reasons for Moule's suicide are treated in some detail, sympathetically and convincingly, in Robert Gittings's *Young Thomas Hardy*.)

A gathering of such friends is noteworthy in any community, and Hardy's talent in identifying and seeking out able intelligences and fellow-spirits amounted to a positive genius during these formative years. Their influence was salutary in all kinds of ways; they forced him to intensify his efforts to learn Greek (Hardy continued to read on his own long after Bastow had left for Tasmania); they introduced him to *Essays and Reviews* and a host of unsettling philosophical and theological studies; they regarded literature and the arts seriously; they set a standard against which he measured himself. But by the early 1860s the circle was disintegrating, and to stay in Dorchester was to wither away in repetitive duties. Hence, moving beyond church restoration – which he was later to despise – required that he learn more about 'the art and science of architecture on more advanced lines', i.e. that he move to London. These are especially critical years, from April 1862, when John Norton, a friend of Hicks, introduced him to Arthur Blomfield, son of the 'recently deceased' Bishop of London and a vigorous, commercially astute and humorous-minded man of thirty-three, to July 1867, when failing health forced him to return to his home in Higher Bockhampton. The turmoil and clamour created by the most active intellectuals of a small town faded away before the breathtaking spectacles of what Wordsworth, in *The Prelude*, had described as the 'monstrous ant-hill on the plain':

> What a shock
> For eyes and ears! what anarchy and din,
> Barbarian and infernal, – a phantasma,
> Monstrous in colour, motion, shape, sight, sound!
>
> (VII, 658–8)

The record of Hardy's years in London is swiftly reviewed in the *Life*, and we would like to know much more about them. What did he and Moule talk about during their many interviews? Why was Hardy so reticent about the details of his professional work (surely nothing embarrassingly personal was involved)? What were Hardy's critical judgements in the 'short addresses or talks on poets and poetry' that he gave to Blomfield's staff on slack afternoons, and did the possibility of lecturing for a living hold an attraction for him then? But it is clear that even without answers to these questions, or to the natural inquiry as to how his relationships with women were managed (he danced at several balls at Willis's Rooms), London proved to be mind-expanding in several crucial ways. Hardy's interest in the theatre, for example, developed rapidly and intensely; he actually appeared at Covent Garden in a pantomime ('The Forty Thieves') and, apparently on another occasion, 'in a representation of the Oxford and Cambridge boat-race'; toyed with the idea of acting 'as a super-numerary for six or twelve months' until closer examination of 'stage realities' disillusioned him; admired Samuel Phelps's Shakespearean productions at Drury Lane; attended several readings by Charles Dickens, which of course were skilful theatrical productions in themselves; enjoyed Charles Kean and his wife (Princess's Theatre), J. B. Buckstone (Haymarket), operas by Rossini, Donizetti, Verdi, Meyerbeer, and Bellini, as well as works staged by the English Opera Company (Hardy 'patrioti-cally' supported the latter, a word which implies that he liked them less); and even thought of writing plays in blank verse.

Another career that seemed likely as a possibility for the first time was that of professional author, although he neither made an effort to meet practising poets nor worked hard at getting published poems that had earned one or two rejection slips. Indeed, his publication of 'How I Built Myself a House' in *Chambers's Journal* (18 March 1865) – an outgrowth of the 'lessons' he provided Blomfield's pupils, and a light-hearted mingling of an architect's professional insights and a would-be novelist's skill at characterisation – was not immediately followed by comparable productions; and Hardy, in later years, was to belittle his first published piece as uncharacteristic and perhaps even as juvenilia (it is better reading than that). He read so much English poetry that he failed to give sufficient attention to the French classes taught by Professor Stiévenard at King's College, and he certainly wrote a great deal of his own; much was to be reclaimed in later years and revised for *Wessex Poems* in 1898, as well as for later volumes. But Hardy realised that he could not live by the money a full-time poet might receive, and combining the careers of poet and architect – for example, as an art critic for the press, specialising in architectural art – seemed unpromising too; as a consequence he brooded on the possibility of 'a scheme of a highly visionary character ... the idea of combining poetry and the Church – towards which he had long had a leaning.' To this end he wrote to Cambridge (probably to Charles Moule), asking for information about matriculation. He foresaw no difficulty: his classical studies had prepared him well. The ultimate goal would be 'a curacy in a country village', where, presumably, his duties would be so arranged that he would have time left over for the writing of more poetry.

The scheme fell through, and we do not know to what extent Hardy prepared the needed credentials for application; but the problem lay not in any feelings of inadequacy but because 'a conscientious feeling, after some theological study', persuaded him 'that he could hardly take the step with honour while holding the views which on examination he found himself to hold'.[7] He confessed to his sister Mary that the service at a Roman Catholic chapel, built by Pugin, had been 'very impressive' (17 August 1862), when he attended it with 'H. M. M.' Efforts to 'practise orthodoxy', sometimes by attendance at Westminster Abbey, proved unavailing. A serious examination of Newman's *Apologia*, undertaken because of Moule's admiration for Newman himself, led to the conclusion: 'Style charming, and his logic really human, being based not on syllogisms but on converging probabilities. Only – and here comes the fatal catastrophe – there is no first link to his excellent chain of reasoning, and down you come headlong.'[8] From Newman Hardy turned to Horace, Byron (*Childe Harold*) and Moore (*Lalla Rookh*), apparently with some relief.

That is to say, Hardy discovered that what had been matter for debate in Dorchester was now settled by experience and reflection in London; he would never again think of himself as 'churchy', as if a career within the church were a possibility. London also made possible the improvement of his understanding of the interrelationships of the visual arts, a matter of some concern to many of his fictions in the following decade.

A curious story about his visits to the National Galley, recorded in the *Life*, stresses the way in which he would confine 'his attention to a single master on each visit', and forbid 'his eyes to stray to any other'.

London, all in all, seems to have fascinated and disappointed Hardy, for there are distinct traces of a restless but undirected ambition, a dissatisfaction that so little of worth had been accomplished by his middle twenties, some unhappiness that his literary efforts had not overwhelmed editors. ('The world does not despise us', he wrote in April, 1865; 'it only neglects us.') Perhaps he did not feel regret so much as understanding and acceptance of the end of another phase in his life when Blomfield, alarmed by his pallor, suggested that 'he should go into the country for a time to regain vigour'. Hardy did not know at the time whether he preferred to 'go into the country altogether'. But it was certain that he would return to Dorchester a different man; that he could never, in one sense, go home again.

What marriage might have been like if the relationship to Tryphena Sparks had ever gone forward, we may only speculate; but it is likely that adjustments that a poor man must make if he is to gain and keep the respect of his lady would have been considerably fewer in such a relationship than were required for the binding of marriage ties between Hardy and Emma Lavinia Gifford. More will be said in another chapter about the human and emotional problems of that relationship, particularly as perceived after Emma's death. For the moment, however, the differences between social stations – perhaps more acute in Emma's and Hardy's imaginations than anyone else's – must be examined. It would be wrong to attribute to Emma alone the energising of the impulse that led to Hardy's devoting so much time to the dramatising of the problem. Readings and reflections on the significance of Darwinian teaching during the 1860s led to more than one sombre anti-romantic document like the poem 'Heiress and Architect', which Hardy dated 1867 and enigmatically dedicated 'For A. W. Blomfield'. He sought ways of curing his own 'despair'. In December 1870, he was struck by the lines in *Hamlet*, 'Thou wouldst not think how ill all's here about my heart: but 'tis no matter.' Social distinctions were always fascinating, but in a world where the race was to the swift, and Hardy moved fumblingly ahead while men of lesser talents succeeded more swiftly, they could be exasperating and self-poisoning, too. In a mordant note dated 15 October 1870, Hardy wrote: 'In a worldly sense it is a matter for regret that a child who has to earn a living should be born of a noble nature. Social greatness requires bitterness to inflate and float it, and a high soul may bring a man to the workhouse.' This, less a generalisation than a personal statement, has patently been formulated by a man who thinks of himself as 'a high soul'.

In three ways Hardy's marriage may be seen as decisively changing his concept of class: his muted but profoundly sensitive reaction to Emma's assumption of superior refinement, an assumption based on her family background; his imaginative works, which refracted the theme of a foredoomed cutting-across social lines for the sale of marriage which would eternise romantic infatuation; and his growing taste for mixing socially with members of the upper classes. There is no need to linger over any of these. Nevertheless, the pattern created by the interweaving of all three is not sufficiently understood by critics who treat the novels as artistic documents largely independent of the circumstances relevant to biography, and it is difficult to appreciate the kind of human being Hardy had become by the time of the death of Emma unless some such review is undertaken.

At one late moment in their relationship (24 April 1910), Emma wrote to Lady Hoare that her husband resembled 'men in general' because, owning intellect and power, he unfortunately lacked 'judgment of ordinary matters', suffered from an egocentric view of the universe, and ought not to be trusted in offices such as that of a magistrate. By then, of course, the marriage ties had rotted more than half away; but long before she met Hardy she had thought of herself as the child of an environment filled with pleasant amenities, as blood-related to picturesque, larger-than-life-size men and women who appreciated her 'sentimental kind of mind', and as truly devout: 'I always loved to hear the chimes', she wrote about St Andrews in Plymouth,

> and admired the beautiful old church which was large and untouched, with grand monuments and large vestibule at the west end now merged in the body of the interior, and which had two huge open grates with well-kept up fires in winter time, giving a most warm and comfortable effect; and a very imposing sight it was to see, and be one, of the large congregation passing out through it.[9]

Though her father drank and did so heavily after any 'wedding, removal, or death' in the family, she remembered him in later years as 'altogether a well-read man with a good memory for literary anecdotes', one who loved Latin and quoted Shakespeare; nor could she wholly condemn him for his violent disapproval of her architect-suitor, since, almost instinctively, she appreciated the reasons for his attitude. Surely Hardy knew that her father called him a 'base churl', or at the very least regarded him as one; his marriage was undertaken without Mr Gifford's blessing; Emma had to visit her brother in London as 'country cousin', and be married at St Peter's Church, Paddington, by her uncle, the Canon of Worcester Cathedral.

For several years marriage proved to be less social, less exciting, than she had romanticised it as being in her anticipations. Surbiton, Bournemouth, Swanage, and Yeovil were quiet retreats, not a series of invitations to the dance. To be sure, moments of happiness flared up, and the uncharitable attitude taken by many toward Emma's memory may well be due to the fact that Hardy has given his personal suffering an attractive literary form, while Emma's unhappiness comes to us through the records of others, and remains intractably anecdotal and unflattering save in a few personal notes; the marriage relationship may have been more serene and attractive – at least until the mid-1880s – than is currently believed, though the religious antagonisms, the increasingly long list of unmentionable subjects at the dinner table, and the jealousies over Hardy's graciousness toward other women were relentlessly building up. Nevertheless, Max Gate, ostensibly Hardy's home to do with as he wished, was not suitable for visits from Hardy's parents or Hardy's sisters, Mary and Kate. At least so notes Carl Weber:

> Hardy's first novel, unpublished, had been called 'The Poor Man and the Lady'. Now that the Poor Man had become a comfortably well-to-do man, able to build himself a house, it was understood that the Lady would have nothing to do with the Poor Man's family. *He* could go to see the dwellers in the cottage at Higher Bockhampton, but he would go alone. Hardy made weekly visits call on his parents, but there is no record of Mrs. Emma Hardy's having ever invited them to Max Gate.[10]

And even Hardy's brother Henry was 'used' rather than welcomed; Emma may have appreciated best his talents as carpenter.

The evidence for judging Hardy's reaction to his wife's easy assumption that her innate good breeding was superior to his exists primarily in poems where veiled statements intimate the existence of varying degrees of resentment. But this is inadequate if we separate it from other kinds of evidence that suggest Hardy accepted a dark reading of his own family past. Frank R. Southerington has performed useful service in reviewing genealogical records (Appendix A, 'The "Family Curse"', in *Hardy's Vision of Man*); Hardy's review of ancestral records 'genuinely disturbed' the novelist, in terms of what he found, 'and perhaps still more by what he conjectured'. Though we cannot at this date interpret with surety how Hardy interpreted the bare facts about his pedigree, as revealed by the local records that he either discovered himself or had pointed out to him by Alfred Pope (close friend and editor of the *Dorset Suits*), we now know that Hardy deliberately obfuscated the facts about his ancestors' relationship to the late Earl of Ilchester, his parents' marriage only five and a half months before his own birth, and a number of other events that occupy the opening pages of the *Life*. If, as Southerington speculates, Hardy's sensitivity to the implications of his own past 'may account in part for the reticence and shyness which marked his whole career' – and that conclusion in itself is modestly stated – it may also account for Hardy's unwillingness to rise up against Emma and state, in proud and unequivocal terms, that his yeoman ancestry counted as much in the eyes of God as the genteel forebears of his West Country wife.

Hardy's fictions keep returning to the problems of family pride carried to excess – a malign influence affecting efforts to live sanely in the modern world – so obsessively that we need mention only a few of the more prominent relationships that illustrate the point. In *Desperate Remedies* Edward Springrove's family background ('a man of rather humble origin', 'the son of a farmer, or something of the kind') is described as a clue to his ambitious character, as a mode of explanation for his desire to get ahead; also, the sinister aspects of illegitimacy are touched on more than once (Aeneas Manston, for example). The father of Elfride, in *A Pair of Blue Eyes*, is not only a bankrupt but a snob who (like Emma's father) is embittered toward Stephen Smith, Elfride's suitor, because the young man's social status is inferior. Disparities between class are as notorious in *The Hand of Ethelberta* (1876), and commented on with as much bitterness, as they seem to have been in *The Poor Man and the Lady*, written almost a full decade earlier; family origins are disguised; in marriage, love is a consideration secondary to security of the family (Pinion[11] uses the term 'careerism' to describe Ethelberta's motivation). The viscount – decadent and disreputable – who marries Ethelberta is part of England's 'useless lumber . . . that'll be the first to burn if there comes a flare'. (One may compare the situation of Ethelberta with that of Geraldine Allenville in 'An Indiscretion in the Life of an Heiress', which Hardy shortened from its original version in *The Poor Man and the Lady*: Geraldine would have sacrificed herself in marriage for the sake of her family, while Ethelberta's brother and father, appalled at the mismatch, seek unsuccessfully to prevent the wedding from taking place.)

Dreary as the melodramatics of *A Laodicean* seem to us today, a large fraction of whatever power the character of William Dare possesses derives from his status as an outsider, his illegitimacy. The mysteriousness with which society recognises and approves the energy of one social climber and condemns the efforts of another self-made man – the different fates met by Farfrae and by Henchard in *The Mayor of Casterbridge* – is only partially explained by the dictum of Novalis, that 'Character is destiny'. If J. O. Bailey is correct in noting that the prefix 'Fitz-' has historically connoted illegitimacy, the infidelity of Fitzpiers in *The Woodlanders* becomes understandable in a context far more interesting than that of the popular fiction of Hardy's age (one critic has written, 'The very name "Edred Fitzpiers" symbolises the conventional cigar-smoking Victorian libertine'[12]); he is fated to some such liaison as that which develops with Felice Charmond; the defect of character runs hot within his blood, and has been transmitted by earlier generations. Nor would Grace Melbury have married Fitzpiers if mistaken notions of the close relationship between virtue and social rank – the class-consciousness of the lady contemplating with disdain the prospect of marriage to a Poor Man like Giles Winterborne – had not affected her judgement (as well as that of her father). As for *Tess of the d'Urbervilles*, that novel is filled with reflections on the influence of heredity, beginning with Simon Stoke's researches at the British Museum – in 'the pages of works devoted to extinct, half-extinct, obscured, and lost families appertaining to the quarter of England in which he proposed to settle' – and continuing relentlessly thereafter as a record of disasters created by an unwarranted sense of family pride. Simon Stoke's family tree may have been a 'work of imagination', but it was no less deadly because of that.

Of the 5041 letters preserved in Hardy's estate after Hardy's own destruction of unwanted correspondence in 1919 and the bonfire of Hardyana fed by the second Mrs Hardy in 1928, no letters from the 'noble dames' who lionised Hardy from the mid-1880s on have survived: Lady Portsmouth, the Duchess of Abercorn, Lady Hilda Broderick, the Marchioness of Londonderry.[13] Yet Hardy carried on an extensive correspondence with members of the landed gentry, and references to all these ladies, and many others of social distinction, may be found in his letters to Emma. One scholar interprets Hardy's protestations of how aware he was of his 'privilege' in writing to Mrs Henniker – which some readers might think was carried to an extreme, considering the worldwide reputation Hardy had achieved by the time he met her – as being traceable to sensitivity over how Emma might react to his friendship with an intellectually worthy and beautiful woman. Perhaps so; and yet Mrs Henniker did move in a different social environment, one that Hardy had always portrayed as glittering and magnificent even when he satirised it in his earlier fictions. The scholar, uneasily and almost unwillingly, recognises a characteristic in these final years: 'what one might almost call his snobbism'. The 'recital of aristocratic names', his 'familiar chit-chat' about titled ladies, his preening of feathers because he has been asked to dine with peers and peeresses, may be found in the letters, and indeed, 'reveal a side of Hardy that does not accord with those other aspects of his nature that have delighted us'.[14] Moreover, Weber, toward the end of his life, apologised for giving wide currency to the notion that Hardy disliked social engagements and attended dinner-parties and teas primarily because Emma urged him to accept invitations; that he tried 'to slip away as soon as possible'. As the correspondence with Emma clearly indicates, Hardy enjoyed the social functions, and Emma often preferred to stay at home in Max Gate:

> When he was alone in London, Hardy was quite ready, at a
> moment's notice to accompany Mrs. Crackanthorpe to the theatre,
> to be summoned to the dinner-table of Lady St. Helier, or to the
> tea-table of the Duchess of Abercorn. These letters show how
> incredibly willing he was to waste his time. In short, *he* was the
> socially-minded one.[15]

The judgement seems unnecessarily harsh. For a creative writer of Hardy's proved integrity and dedication to craft, social diversions, even amongst the aristocracy, must not be resented as diversions from the channelling of creative energies to the service of Literature. Ultimately it may not be possible to guess either the extent of the uses Hardy made of his social experiences, or the quality of the writing he might have produced had he stayed behind the barricade of walls and growing trees erected at Max Gate. But what happened as these invitations multiplied, as Hardy's fame grew, as letters bearing the stamps of fifty nations cascaded through the mailbox, could not have done anything less than accelerate the process of alienation from Dorchester's ways of thinking that had begun in the early 1860s. Hardy lived in Dorchester and wrote about its people and its history all his life; yet increasingly he thought of it as part of a wider world, of Wessex; and if he imposed his concept of a timeless Casterbridge upon the imaginations of the reading public (as all great artists ultimately do with their personal visions), it may be remarked, in passing, that he did the same to himself as well. He, too, became an observer rather than a participant in the local affairs of Dorchester; his keenness of glance, remarked by all visitors to Max Gate, made the natives of Dorchester uneasy not only because they did not appreciate becoming the raw materials of art, but because they suspected, with some rightness, that their habits and standards were being exposed as provincial. The native *had* returned in June 1883; but it became increasingly difficult for residents of Dorchester to think of Hardy as one of themselves.

Over the years since 1958, when J. Stevens Cox began his remarkable series of pamphlets and monographs memorialising the view of everyone who had known Hardy personally (the Toucan Press Monographs and from 1970 onwards the *Thomas Hardy Year Book*), comments expressing resentment and shock at the frequently hostile recollections of Hardy's personality and life-style have turned up in various works of scholarship and criticism. Ephemera these Cox booklets admittedly are; but their consistency, and occasional crankiness, have rendered all admirers of Hardy a genuine service; they make it impossible to sustain the belief that Hardy, in his final years, developed into a tame, tweedy literary idol, content to be adulated, and at peace with either the world or himself. The most important single moment of change must have taken place during 1912, in the midst of the shocked realisation that Emma, stodgy, eccentric in a number of unpleasant ways, and hardly more than a reassuring presence whom he took for granted, would no longer accompany his path through life. If life ever imitates art, as the aesthetes of the 1890s assured their contemporaries, Hardy's reaction to Emma's passing must have been similar to the bishop's shock at Mrs Proudie's death, as recorded in Trollope's *The Last Chronicle of Barset* (1867):

> She had in some ways, and at certain periods of his life, been very good to him. She had kept his money for him and made things go straight, when they had been poor. His interests had always been her interests. Without her he would never have been a bishop. So, at least he told himself now, and so told himself probably with truth. She had been very careful of his children. She had never been idle. She had never been fond of pleasure. She had neglected no acknowledged duty. He did not doubt that she was now on her way to heaven. He took his hands from his head, and clasping them together, said a little prayer. It may be doubted whether he quite knew for what he was praying. The idea of praying for her soul, now that she was dead, would have scandalised him. He certainly was not praying for his own soul. I think he was praying that God might save him from being glad that his wife was dead. (Ch. 67, 'In Memoriam')

Yet, as Trollope noted immediately thereafter, the bishop's thoughts toward the woman who had scarred him (as a *thorn* might: both Trollope and Hardy used the word to characterise these women) rapidly became 'very tender to her', because 'Nothing reopens the springs of love so fully as absence, and no absence so thoroughly as that which must needs be endless.' Like the bishop, Hardy wanted that which he had not; and especially that which he could never have. But Emma was not a native of Dorchester, and the memories which surged freshest to the fore were of Cornwall, of *elsewhere*. He had been happiest with Emma before he returned to Dorchester, before he had built Max Gate. The astonishing outburst of lyrical feeling which suffused scores of poems in 1912–13 may be regarded, from our angle of interest in Hardy's final years, as an implicit recognition that the past was retrievable only in fitful moments, and that he must now settle down to a widower's existence.

Florence Emily Dugdale, a much more colourless personality than Emma, was *there* when Hardy needed her, and Hardy's marriage to her, on 10 February 1914, must be recognised as an effort to minimise the loneliness of his life, now in its seventy-third year, and to eliminate any possibility of scandal in their relationship. It was a marriage of convenience, however much we stress the instinct for beauty and charm that informs her several books written for children. Florence was less than half his age; her research for *The Dynasts* – conducted at his request, and under his instructions, at the British Museum – was part of a continuing series of businesslike arrangements that began immediately after Mrs Henniker's introduction of Miss Dugdale to Hardy in 1904. He needed someone to handle routine correspondence and save him from troublesome invaders of his privacy; his energies, after all, were limited, and he could not cope with all the comings and goings that would have destroyed his working day if somebody had not performed the necessary tasks that Florence undertook willingly, and with increasing efficiency. She served as secretary; she ran the household; and her duties, particularly after Emma's death, made it impossible for her to move around Dorset as freely as she had been used to.

All of Hardy's poems written for or about her speak of gratitude and appreciation of what she was doing for him; but she was not a second Emma, she knew it, and she must have resented it as, over the years, Hardy kept recurring, in his thoughts and poems, to events that had taken place before she was born. And it is probable that Florence consented to the sensational division of heart from body that marked the circumstances of Hardy's final return to dust and ashes because Hardy, in his will, had asked 'if possible' to be buried 'in my wife Emma's grave' – a desire that could neither be ignored nor be pleasing to Florence – while, at the request of the nation and with the concurrence of the Dean of Westminster, he might also be buried in the Poets' Corner of the Abbey.

Florence's desire, after Hardy's death, was to see him honoured among his peers. Indeed, his pallbearers were to include the Prime Minister, Stanley Baldwin; and Rudyard Kipling, George Bernard Shaw, James Barrie, John Galsworthy, A. E. Housman, and Edmund Gosse. As through the final years of his life she had sought to ease his way, protect his privacy, humour his whims, and further his reputation, so in the funeral rites did she arrange for the national honours that she believed to be his due. She contributed the final four chapters (those treating the decade 1918–28) to *The Later Years of Thomas Hardy* – the second half of the 'biography' that Hardy for the most part wrote himself in the form of rough copy' – and made the arrangements for the Hardy Memorial Room to be established in the Dorset County Museum. Richard Little Purdy has dedicated his splendid bibliographical study of Thomas Hardy to 'F. E. H. in affectionate remembrance'. Many admirers of Hardy owe her a large debt of gratitude, for she helped all scholars once she was assured that their interest in her late husband's memory was respectful and sincere. But between Hardy and Florence the relationship was solidly sombre in hue, and we have no evidence that Florence, as a woman, reminded the ageing poet of the mercurial, unsettling passions of Emma. Hardy's infatuation with Mrs Gertrude Bugler, a beautiful actress who played the roles of his heroines in dramatised versions of his novels, took place when he was fully eighty-four; Florence suffered from a flare-up of jealousy; but her husband's feeling for Mrs Bugler was short-lived, even though exasperatingly unexpected. (In fairness to Mrs Bugler, she did not realise what havoc she had wrought in Hardy's heart or at Hardy's dinner table.)

Sympathy for the hard lot of Florence – a favorite theme in Dorchester gossip even to this day – may distract us from awareness of limitations in her personality that made unlikely the formation of any genuinely romantic relationship. She let the occasional wretchedness of her circumstances be known among friends; she occasionally bullied servants; she often yielded to Hardy's wishes when it was not necessary to do so. But it is doubtful that Hardy would have changed much in these years even if Florence's personality had been quite different; and as she was, she suited him.

He continued to be an 'Intrinsicalist', favouring 'social readjustments rather than social subversions – remembering that the opposite of error is error still'.[16] In large measure trained by the standards of the preceding century, he thought that the study of history could explain the confusing trends of the post-war world.[17] He continued to subscribe to, and propagandise for, a few socially liberal and humanitarian causes: more flexible divorce laws for one,[18] and better treatment for animals as another.[19] Day after day he went to his desk at ten o'clock, intending to work. In the words of Newman Flower:

> It was a discipline which he had carried out through the years. Maybe he would not write a word for a fortnight or longer. Then one morning the mood would come to him and he would work strongly through part of the day. The ritual of the daily attendance at his desk which was more often than not abortive, was necessary to his life.[20]

Slowly, carefully, he assembled the contents of his five books of verse during this period, and published them for the benefit of a relatively small, but gratifyingly faithful, audience. To those who visited him – and he could count among his personal friends the best writers of the still-continuing Edwardian afterglow, and many younger post-war writers who admired him – he extended a cordial, dignified hospitality, and was apt to smile inwardly rather than laugh aloud when the conversation turned humorous. Sometimes he did not devote his entire attention to the voices of those who came to tea. What William Archer recorded shortly after the turn of the century, a statement made by Hardy, was what Hardy continued to believe as his years dwindled down to winter words:

> But for my part I say in all sincerity, 'Better be inconvenienced by visitants from beyond the grave than see none at all.' The material world is so uninteresting, human life is so miserably bounded, circumscribed, cabin'd, cribb'd, confined. I want another domain for the imagination to expatiate in.[21]

And, as subsequent chapters will show, he became increasingly convinced that his efforts to support reform movements in liturgy revision, organisations that might eliminate quarrels between nations, and humanitarian societies would be ultimately futile. The long night was settling down. Even though he had previsioned it, his thoughts about human nature locked in hopeless struggle with a Will that did not even know the damage it wrought (during these years he even disdained to write God with a capital letter) became more cheerless and mordant than when he had been censured by critics and reviewers in the 1880s and 1890s for holding 'pessimistic' views.

The Child is father of the Man: links of continuity between the boy Tom who, at the age of eight or nine, first visited London and was impressed by 'the pandemonium of Smithfield, with its mud, curses, and cries of ill-treated animals'[22] and the elderly gentleman who fought with formidable rhetorical skills against blood sports and cruelty to animals are easily traced. But it is the Ancient speaking not only to other Ancients, but to his contemporaries and indeed to us, whom we must now follow.

2

Emma

The privacy of Thomas Hardy was jealously guarded, and increasingly so during the final decades. It was entirely to be expected: much as he enjoyed social life, dinner parties, conversations among friends, and the chances to encourage younger writers, still, he was ageing; he did not always feel well; he had his own work to do; and there was the continual sorting through the detritus of a lifetime, the discarding of what was no longer wanted. He needed more time to lock himself away from a prying public than even four score and upward might allow.

Nevertheless, our survey of Hardy's final years must begin with a consideration of an essentially private matter, the author's relationship to his first wife, Emma Lavinia Gifford. That relationship began on 7 March 1870. Hardy, a thirty-year old architect who had already served his six-year apprenticeship under John Hicks, an architect practising in Dorchester, met her after travelling to St Juliot, N. Cornwall, to assist in the reconstruction of the church there. Emma – half a year younger than Hardy – was then living with her sister, Helen Catherine, and Helen's husband, the Reverend Caddell Holder, the rector of St Juliot. Hardy fell instantly in love with her – for reasons that we shall examine shortly – and enjoyed her company on various excursions. She copied and recopied manuscripts for him. He used Cornish localities (St Juliot rectory, Boscastle, Beeny Cliff) as background for *A Pair of Blue Eyes*, which he began to write in 1871 after the unenthusiastic reception of his first published novel, *Desperate Remedies*. Despite the disapproval of John Attersoll Gifford, Emma's father – a retired solicitor – and his own uncertain financial prospects, Hardy became more certain that he wanted to marry Emma. The genuine success of *Far from the Madding Crowd* – published serially (and anonymously) in the *Cornhill Magazine* during 1874 – persuaded the young author that the time had come to marry. The ceremony took place at St Peter's, Paddington, rather than in Cornwall, a fact which justifies the assumption that even on the wedding-day (17 September 1874) John Gifford believed his daughter was marrying beneath her social station; nor did Hardy's success as a novelist ever lead to more than grudging acceptance from John Gifford, who died in 1890.

The marriage lasted thirty-eight years, and ended only with Emma's death on 27 November 1912, at Max Gate. Both parties remained untouched by scandal. We have no reason to believe that Hardy, despite his courtesies toward the fair sex (he was something of a ladies' man), and despite Emma's occasional flare-ups of jealousy, ever strayed. It was a complex relationship. Several elements in that marriage must remain forever undefined and murky. We cannot be certain of the reasons why Emma disliked Hardy's family: it is possible to build too heavy a superstructure on the known facts that the author went by himself to his parents weekly (they did not come to Max Gate), and that Mary and Kate – Hardy's sisters – never came to the Wareham Road to visit their brother. We do not know whether Hardy complained about his wife's behaviour to Mrs Arthur Henniker, a talented, 'charming, *intuitive*' woman whom he greatly admired; who shared many interests with him; and who, in 1920, even entertained the notion of buying a house to be near Max Gate. But, above all, we do not know what Emma knew about Tryphena Sparks.

For that matter, we do not know much about Tryphena. The controversy about Tryphena's relationship with Thomas Hardy is obscured by the faultiness of memories in an ageing woman; Tryphena's eldest daughter, Mrs Eleanor Tryphena Brommell, was in her middle eighties when interviewed in the 1960s by Miss Lois Deacon, and was attempting to recall what her mother had said to her some eight decades earlier. She had little to offer in the way of direct documentation. Hardy never mentioned Tryphena in his autobiography, and referred to her directly in only the one poem 'Thoughts of Phena', which cannot bear the burden of over-interpretation or wild surmise.

The facts are simple enough. Tryphena was a native of Puddletown, a cousin of Hardy (her mother was the elder sister of Hardy's mother), and – in 1869–71 – a student at Stockwell Training College for teachers in London. After that, she became the headmistress of a Public Free School, an elementary school for girls in Plymouth. In 1877 she married Charles Gale; helped serve at the bar of her husband's hotel in Topsham (near Exeter); bore four children; and died in 1890 when her eldest child was eleven.

Was she engaged to Hardy? Mrs Bromell believed so. Miss Irene Cooper Willis, a good friend of the second Mrs Hardy and the lawyer for the Trustees of Hardy's estate, has spoken, on the basis of a conversation with Florence Emily, of the existence of a 'discarded maiden'. A number of piquant and otherwise unidentified allusions to a woman other than Emma turn up in both the fiction and the poems. But for the same reasons that make unreliable any effort to reconstruct biography from first-person statements in lyrical poems, the ingenious 'readings' of several of Hardy's poems, used to justify and document a host of hypotheses, raise legitimate suspicions that a poet's mind does not simply transfer events of his own life to nakedly confessional poetry. A romantic involvement, and even an engagement, seem easier to accept than the theory that Hardy introduced Tryphena to Horace Moule, but kept the fact of his engagement a secret; that Tryphena and Horace fell in love with each other in 1869–70; that Hardy knew what happened, but did not break his engagement. And some claims are even more extravagant: Hardy is assumed to have been responsible for Tryphena's illegitimate child 'Randy', who – ignorant of his father's true identity – was sent off to Bristol to live with Tryphena's brother. The identification of Randy as a teenage boy in a photograph was made by Mrs Brommell shortly before she died, but we have no supporting documentation of Randy's birth in any register thus far consulted. Florence Emily told Miss Willis that Hardy broke off the engagement with Tryphena, and then gave Emma the ring Tryphena had returned to him; but, again, only the Scottish verdict 'Not proven' seems an appropriate response.

But let us return to a romance we know more about, that between Hardy and his first wife. Our interest in the romance is legitimate, even though the fact of Hardy's privacy is so well attested. Emma was crucial to Hardy's poetry, particularly after her death. In more than one hundred poems – at least an eighth of his total poetical production, exclusive of *The Dynasts* – she figures as inspiration, and often as failed goddess. The most private of emotions are carefully recorded in lyrics that he published during his lifetime. He invited the world to study that relationship, and though he disguised events, changed names, and sometimes buried the meaning of a moment at an irretrievable depth, the major outlines of what Emma meant to him are clear enough, and surely were to those who knew Hardy personally.

Inevitably Emma saw herself, her husband, and her husband's friends, differently from the way in which much of the rest of the world must have seen those same relationships. The passing of time has not, in general, been kind to her memory, though the editing by Evelyn Hardy and Robert Gittings of Emma's personal manuscript, *Some Recollections* (London: Oxford University Press, 1961), has provided the full document from which Hardy borrowed nine pages for *The Early Life of Thomas Hardy*, and has made possible clearer perception of the attractive elements in Emma's personality. (Hardy, after all, used only those comments made by her which related to himself.)

Emma's fastidious distaste for the omnibuses of London ('a very un-dignified method of getting about') was consistent with another passage that Hardy omitted, written on the second page of her reminiscences: 'My home was a most intellectual one and not only so but one of exqui-site home-training and refinement – alas the difference the loss of these amenities and gentlenesses has made to me!' Visitors to Max Gate were appalled at her shallowness, her lack of interest in (and sometimes her distaste for) her husband's projects, her superciliousness; Rebecca West once heard her say, 'Try to remember, Thomas Hardy, that you married a lady!' George Gissing spoke of her as 'an extremely silly & discontented woman' in a letter written to his brother on 25 September 1895. And Carl Weber, usually the most discreet of biographers, was unable to mask his irritation at the way Emma refused to allow her husband to ride in her carriage 'up the steep hill' to the Royal Garden Party at Windsor Castle on 22 June 1907. Emma preferred to have Madame Blanche, wife of a French portrait-painter, ride with her:

> The latter declined, urging Hardy to take the seat and spare himself in the July-like heat. The author had just passed his sixty-seventh birthday and looked even older. Rheumatism had so lamed his back that on a previous occasion he had found it impossible to walk down-stairs. He was obviously frail. Other guests headed for Windsor Castle followed Madame Blanche's example in urging Hardy to ride. But Mrs. Hardy settled the matter. 'Mr. Hardy ride? That walk up the hill in the sun will do him a lot of good.' So up the stony hill Thomas Hardy and his portrait-painter trudged on foot, following the open carriage with its driver in King Edward's scarlet livery and its lady in a green veil, seated under a bright silk umbrella.[1]

Florence Dugdale wrote an angry letter to Edward Clodd on 13 January 1913 (and never changed her mind about Emma): 'Of course nothing can be more lonely than the life he used to lead – long evenings spent alone in his study, insult & abuse his only enlivenment! It sounds cruel to write like that, & in atrocious taste, but truth is truth, after all.'[2] The testimony of all these witnesses is remarkably consistent, and has left us with a series of remarkably unflattering images, perhaps none crueller than that left behind by Gertrude Atherton, who described Emma, at the home of the Duchess of Sutherland, as 'an excessively plain, dowdy, high-stomached woman with her hair drawn back in a tight little knot'.

Yet even this bill of indictment does not include all the reasons why

Hardy lived palely, and perhaps even miserably, under the same roof with her. There was, for one thing, the chasm which separated their religious convictions: hers orthodox and conventional; respectable; inelastic and unforgiving; while his, which had long since rejected the institutionalised faith of his contemporaries, might best be characterised as brooding, sombre, and for the most part unhopeful. Clive Holland has left us one of many records of how Emma attempted to neutralise Hardy's 'unorthodox views upon conventional Christianity and his abhorrence of religious pretensions which had no counterpart in the actual lives of the people making them', because she was shocked and worried lest word of his unorthodoxy get abroad:

> Next morning (Holland) received – as he did on several other occasions – a note from Mrs. Hardy, stating that she hoped that neither he or her visitor would regard what her husband said on religious matters as serious, adding the information that he regularly read his Greek Testament.[3]

Moreover, she was jealous of Hardy's writing talent. Without her encouragement, he might not have forsaken the profession of architecture to take up the uncertainties of a writing career; but that period when she defied her father's distaste of her suitor, encouraged her husband as helpmeet, wrote out his manuscripts at tedious length (and recopied them), and contributed ideas that helped shape scenes in his novels, had largely ended by the mid-1880s. She deluded herself that she had served as the model for *Tess*. Appalled by Hardy's convictions – which inevitably were refracted by his fictions – she attempted to have him soften or delete passages from the books that he was writing, and inevitably she was rebuffed – how unkindly, we cannot say; but there can be no doubt that Hardy was his own man, determined never to degenerate into a writer who would take 'a broker's view of his heroine and her adornments'.[4] He would not flatter the preconceptions of Mrs Grundy; he would not pander to what, in his essay 'Candour in English Fiction', he called 'English prudery'. And it outraged Emma that violations of decency and of what she considered a proper respect for the opinions of mankind should be rewarded by great commercial success for her husband. One of the saddest events in all Victorian literary history was the trip taken by Emma to London – after her husband had refused to make changes in the manuscript of *Jude the Obscure* – to appeal to Richard Garnett, of the British Museum, that he in turn might exert pressure on her recalcitrant husband. This time she wanted more than deletions or alterations; she wept because Dr Garnett would not ask her husband to *burn* the entire manuscript. Those who frequented the British Museum soon knew of Emma's appeal, and it seems unlikely that Hardy could have remained ignorant of his wife's intervention.

Emma may have believed her own literary abilities offered competition to those of her husband, but 'Spring Song' and' 'Trumpet Call', 'The Gardener's Ruse' and 'Dancing Maidens' are jejune when compared even to a Hardy poem written in a moment of weak inspiration. The *Dorset County Chronicle* might publish a lyric as an effusion of a local resident, or Clement K. Shorter might print a lyric in the *Sphere* as an acknowledgement of respect for her husband's talents; but Emma's book *Alleys*, published in Dorchester by F. G. Longman in 1911, exhibits an amiable but essentially uninteresting optimism about flowers and birds, and the doggerel is painfully mawkish. And what is one to say about her 'Exposition of Great Truths', contained in the companion prose volume *Spaces*? This speaks of 'The High Delights of Heaven' and of 'ease of locomotion'; the distinction between 'Acceptors and Non-Acceptors'; the 'Last Day', with the miraculous appearance, in the east, of 'a spot of light . . . at 4 o'clock a.m. according to western time – and dark night of Eastern time or about that hour'; and a final 'Retrospect'. It is all perfervid, a disconcerting jumble of the literal and the unreal.

Ultimately, no doubt, it was harmless enough, but Emma's complete sanity in the final decade of her life had been questioned not only by those who resented the intolerable burden she laid upon her (largely uncomplaining) husband, but by the citizens of Dorchester, most of whom knew little or nothing about the nature of the domestic household. Evelyn L. Evans has written that Emma 'was considered very odd by the townspeople, who would touch their foreheads significantly as she went by, free-wheeling on her bicycle, with her feet off the pedals.'[5] Hardy himself once referred, in a letter to Mrs Arthur Henniker dated 17 December 1912, to 'certain painful delusions she suffered at times', and these hallucinations are nowhere clearly described. (J. O. Bailey suggests that 'At a Fashionable Dinner', which has obvious connections with the third stanza of 'The Interloper', comes close to defining the nature of Emma's delusions.[6] In the former poem Lavine [Emma] is asked by her husband to describe the meaning of an elongated shade 'by a distant screen', and answers that it is like her own body lying beyond the door: 'And it means my death hour! –' Hardy objects that the sight reminds him more of 'satin sheen'. But she, persistently morbid, tells her husband that his interpretation means, in turn, that his new bride, when he wins her, will wear satin at her wedding: 'It's her satin dress, no doubt

– / That shine you see – / My own corpse to me!') That these hallucinations were only occasional, never completely disabling, and not what Hardy or any of us would want to remember about Emma, seems worth repeating. Even the addition of the line 'And I saw the figure and visage of Madness seeking for a home' to 'The Interloper' in the 1923 edition of *Collected Poems* does not mean that Hardy believed his wife had gone over the brink. It is true that 'The Interloper' does deal with insanity. Though we may discount some of Florence Emily's bitterness about her predecessor, there really was in the Gifford family a wide streak of what can only charitably be called eccentricity. Hardy, in *Moments of Vision*, was sufficiently disturbed by Emma's behaviour to print not only 'The Interloper' but 'At the Piano' and 'The Man with a Past', poems which respectively dealt with 'a cowled Apparition' pushing between a lover and his beloved, and with the grinning of 'the fully bared thing'.

All of these taken together – Emma's sense of social superiority to her husband, her dowdiness in later years, her unwillingness to let her husband alone (she was the classic case of a woman who could neither live with nor without her husband), her literary pretensions, and her erratic behaviour – deepened the gloom at Max Gate. It was not a happy household. Hardy, who had hoped for children to carry on his name (his will speaks poignantly of the child who never came), remained uncomforted by the sound of children's voices. Everything should have conspired to sour the memories of an incompatible wife once she preceded him to the grave at Stinsford.

The fact that her death released memories of how much he had loved her when romance originally flowered in the region of St Juliot is perhaps not surprising in itself, but the homage he paid to her memory continued for so many years that Florence Emily became uneasy at its unnaturalness as extended sorrow, and doubtless felt her own position threatened; the length of time that he mourned is in itself surprising, and the added circumstance of a large number of later poems written to describe the 'division', the reality of permanent misunderstanding, alienation, and growing bitterness at mismatching of temperaments – a circumstance which argues that Hardy, better than any outsider, saw realistically the dimensions of his dilemma – is most surprising of all. It is as if he saw the futility of any idealisation of Emma's character, as if he understood fully the need for accepting his share of responsibility for what went wrong. At the same time he identified those elements in Emma's patterns of living which made friction inevitable, and he still could not help himself, could not prevent his writing both the poems of impassioned reliving of moments long since gone and the poems in which he rendered critical judgement; he was both inside and outside the picture-frame; he was tormented by what a contemporary poet was to term the 'intolerable antilogies' of a situation beyond hope of solution.

For Hardy, certain favourable aspects of Emma's character remained unchanged, though time ravaged her physical appeal and ultimately served to weaken her judgement of how best to live with her husband. *Some Recollections*, as we know, was written late in her life, and it records, with considerable literary skill, vignettes of life at Plymouth and St Juliot. Within its brief compass it breathes an intense appreciation of landscape and the natural world. It provides ample testimony of how observant an eye Emma had for the oddnesses of other people's behaviour. But, above all, it tells us, directly and without the kind of disguise that Hardy often created for moments of self-revelation, what kind of woman Emma was in her sunset years.

She remembered how the sight of daisies put her into an 'ecstatic state'; how independent she was from the very beginning; how 'long garden seats with long tables' and a circular seat encircling 'a magnificent Elm tree of great age and girth' provided for her 'a most delightful spot ... for happy childhood'; how she played recklessly but with great self-confidence along 'the dangerous pathways over cliffs and rocks leading to spots almost inaccessible' at the Hoe; how she enjoyed the rainy days of Plymouth ('of the soft, almost imperceptible-sprinkling kind to which the folk there get used and which produces dewy complexions and patient manners'); how she gloried in dances ('... our hair floated about in the rush of air made by our whirlings'); how she drew a distinction between the gallery of a church (stimulating a 'mild species of gaiety' among young people) and 'the solemn pews'; how immediately and sympathetically she reacted to her father's stagey declamation of Shakespeare; how delighted she was by the Royal Baths of Union Street, Plymouth ('coolness, freshness and saltness'); how she nicely balanced favourable and unfavourable traits of a tame seagull ('He was not particular in his appetite, which was of the gorging kind, and most friendly'); how innocently she admired the market, with its vegetables, flowers, dairy produce, and fish ('shiny beautiful creatures stiff with freshness and marvellously cheap'); how she rebelled against hints of marriage from 'officious' types ('I prefer my mare to any husband'); how she delighted in the spectacular scenery of Tintagel ('the winter waves and foam reaching hundreds of feet up the stern, strong dark rocks with the fantastic revellings of the gulls, puffins and rooks, jackdaws, in attendance, "black souls and white", sometimes called'); how instinctively she reacted to the 'old-time sadness' of the old Abbey at Lanivet ('One's soul was not refreshed out of doors, where we were amongst the bones of the former immured people, though no cemetery could be seen or known'); how – on first seeing the man who was to marry her – she was 'immediately arrested by his familiar appearance', as if she 'had seen him in a dream'; how the ivy 'hung gaily from the roof-timbers' of St Juliot Church; how she relished fortune-telling and 'various queer tales and information'; how she sought continually for 'a dear heart-whole person' in the midst of 'laborious workers, dull, aggressive', who resembled nothing so much as 'the hard nature of the soil, spread out in bareness and stones'; and how, finally, she thought of herself as proceeding through life with 'a strange unearthly brilliance' shining 'around her path'.

It is a character-sketch, complete in itself, of a physically active, observant, and generally good-humoured child maturing into young womanhood; disapproving of her father's drinking 'outbursts', but unable to end them or rescue the declining family fortunes, and conscious that she might have been over-trained in a genteel tradition (Emma gives no indication of why, after six months' experience as a governess, she had no further interest in continuing); shy about expressing feelings, but with strong independently-held likes and dislikes ('I was the only one I believe who liked him', she says of her great Uncle Davie; of the mother of Charles E. Gifford she writes, in a revealing phrase, 'and the first moment I saw her I loved her, though I was not demonstrative about my affection'), even differentiating between 'Cornish working orders' and 'Devonshire folk'.

What Hardy preserved, so far as Emma's allusions to him are concerned (and he evidently destroyed a good deal), is not only a series of 'small details and small events', written down on the assumption that 'some other people may like to have them', but a sense of wonderment, on Emma's part, that romance finally found her out. *Some Recollections* hints at a jealousy of Emma's sister that continued even after the latter became Mrs Holder. There is the striking complacency of Emma's remark about her father's preference for her as 'his only *fair* child with bright hair, which he would stroke with sighings occasionally'; and a later comment about her feeling like an outsider during the welcoming ceremonies for the new bridegroom and bride at St Juliot Church ('Whether they could have expected me I do not know. I remained on the stairs, looking on, much entertained with it all'); and, as revealing as anything else, her saying how strange it was for her to go with her sister and her new husband to St Juliot Rectory, 'considering that my sister had had a jealous feeling towards me ever since I had been grown up.' But it was precisely this move that led to her meeting Thomas Hardy, and to romance sufficient for all of them, and it is not surprising that Hardy, discovering this manuscript, was deeply moved by the story of Ann Tresider Chappel's divination that Emma would marry a writer; the sentence that accompanies her description of the need for church repairs, 'My life's romance now began'; the wonderment, expressed by Emma and shared by her husband, that the circumstances of their meeting should be so unusual, that they should find each other by coming 'together from two different though neighbouring counties to this one at this very remote spot, with beautiful sea-coast, and the wild Atlantic ocean rolling in with its magnificent waves and spray, its white gulls and black choughs and grey puffins, its cliffs and rocks and gorgeous sun-settings sparkling redness in a track widening from the horizon to the shore' (p. 50).

Hardy, described in Emma's sketch variously as 'The Architect' and 'the stranger', turns up as familiar as if she had previsioned him in a dream. He has a 'slightly different accent' and a 'soft voice'. Their con-versation was of books, and of lively topics closed to Emma in a custo-marily sluggish and unenlightened community (or so she felt) – 'I found him a perfectly new subject of study and delight' – and even if Emma assumed too easily more credit than was her due for a creative collabora-tion with the man who was to become her husband – 'we talked much of plots, possible scenes, tales, and poetry and of his own work' – there is nothing inherently implausible in the hypothesis that Hardy did discuss with her his ambitions to become a writer to an extent that he did not do, and perhaps could not do, with anyone else during the courtship period (1870–4).[7] The number of trips taken by Hardy to Cornwall during this same period was not excessive, and Emma speaks of his personal visits to see her as taking place 'two or three times a year'. The gaps between visits were filled by correspondence and the relishing of memories; the intensity of reunions must have been all the keener as a consequence. At any rate, the speculation by the editors of Some Recollections that Emma's 'very silence on the subject of any division between them was a reproach in itself' (p. x) seems reasonably stated; the 'venom, hatred & abuse' with which Emma described her husband and his family (the authority for this statement is Florence Emily Hardy, in a letter to Rebekah Owen, dated 18 January 1916) were reserved for her 'awful diary', which Hardy read, reread, and finally destroyed, so that only the golden memories of Some Recollections remained behind. No one really wishes that the contents of that diary could be reconstructed.

The legacy of poetry which Some Recollections inspired must always be assessed with the fact of Hardy's age at the time of composition in mind. He was, in the year of Emma's death and of the subsequent discovery of her compressed autobiography, a majestic and grizzled seventy-two. But to say this is not preliminary to a characterisation of Hardy's love poems as the impassioned, uncritical, and adoring effusions of an elder who has once again drunk at the fountain of youth. Indeed, Hardy's tracing of the history of his love affair is remarkably objective in important respects. Impulse and emotion are given due credit; poignant questions are asked; final judgements are suspended. Even the sequence in which Hardy's reborn romantic strain sings most clearly, 'Poems of 1912–13', originally published in *Satires of Circumstance, Lyrics and Reveries* (1914), has ambiguous shadings, and there is more than a little sadness in any arrangement of the lyrics that an editor may work out.[8] Virgil's *Veteris vestigia flammae* – relics of the old fire – has ironic overtones in its position as epigraph at the head of these twenty-one poems. For relics can be charred and appallingly fragile, *vulnerable*, as well as precious and much-loved, and Hardy's memories are rueful and bitter-sweet. Unalloyed happiness – the verses of 'When I Set Out for Lyonnesse', printed in *Satires of Circumstance* and one of Hardy's most popular lyrics – is non-existent here. It is not that Hardy falsifies or denies the glamour of the romance which existed in the 1870s because of his knowledge of the pain, misunderstanding, and harshness of what went on as the century aged; but rather that these are poems of a man writing after his wife's death: none has been retrieved from a desk drawer, the original draft of none antedates Emma's death, knowledge of the fact of the *completion* of the romance yellows the edge of every lyric. Thus, 'Beeny Cliff', with its bright immediacy of 'the opal and the sapphire of that wandering western sea' and 'the pale mews plained below us', darkens not only as a consequence of March rain but because the speaker knows that his beloved is 'elsewhere', that she 'nor knows nor cares for Beeny, and will laugh there nevermore.' A woman calls in 'The Voice', even as 'when our day was fair', even as when she wore her 'original air-blue gown', but perhaps it is 'only the breeze', and she has dissolved forever into 'wan listlessness', and can be 'heard no more again far or near'. He remembers climbing the road behind a chaise ('At Castle Boterel'), talking to 'a girlish form', but 'love's old domain' can be traversed 'never again,' and the 'phantom figure'

> Remains on the slope, as when that night
> Saw us alight,

and the speaker, looking back, sees the image 'shrinking, shrinking,' in the rain. And, similarly, in poems like 'The Phantom Horsewoman', when he sees, 'in a careworn craze', the vision of 'a ghost-girl-rider'; and in 'Where the Picnic was', when he returns to the scene of a picnic – where 'the sea breathes brine' – his mood is not so much autumnal as wintry. His beloved 'has shut her eyes / For evermore', the realities of yesterday are 'banished / Ever into nought' ('St. Launce's Revisited'), and 'all's closed now, despite Time's derision' ('After a Journey'). Hardy's recognition that the past yields melancholy thoughts of what might have been, as well as vivid memories of what actually took place, finds expression in the haunting opening line of 'A Dream or No': 'Why go to Saint-Juliot? What's Juliot to me?'

Hardy's effort to define the happiness of his romance with 'dearest Emmie' should not, therefore, be seen as restricted to the poems composed in 1912–13, for quantitatively these poems are only a small fraction of what he had to say about that relationship. Nor did Hardy rest for long with the view expressed in 'Beeny Cliff', that theirs had been a love transcending difficulties and misunderstanding: 'The woman whom I loved so, and who loyally loved me.' Nevertheless, Hardy's own recollections of what he loved most about Emma – her 'bright hair flapping free', 'her delicate head' ('Rain on a Grave'), her swan neck, her 'rose-flush coming and going' ('After a Journey'), and the fearlessness ('Places') with which, on her 'pretty mare Fanny', as Emma had called her,

> She cantered down, as if she must fall
> (Though she never did),
> To the charm of all,

may never have been more intense in the poems he wrote for his later volumes of verse.

> And though, toil-tried,
> He withers daily,
> Time touches her not,
> But she still rides gaily
> In his rapt thought
> On that shagged and shaly
> Atlantic spot,
> And as when first eyed
> Draws rein and sings to the swing of the tide.
>
> ('The Phantom Horsewoman')

Frank Pinion's arrangement of 'the chronological order of the primary experiences which [the poems about Emma] convey'[9] is sensible and trustworthy: the poems that Hardy, immediately after reading *Some*

Recollections, wrote about Emma's early years at Plymouth; his first visit
to St Juliot; subsequent meetings; early years of marriage; outbreaks of
'insanity'; 'the Division'; last years; Emma's death; her grave at Stinsford;
Hardy's pilgrimages; her memorial at St Juliot; recollections (a miscel-
laneous gathering); and 'living bereaved'. Since it is not always clear
whether Hardy is disguising Emma's identity under an indefinite female
pronoun or a second-person direct address, a number of poems other
than those that Pinion identifies are difficult to subsume under these
specific categories. The blooming and subsequent ageing of the romance,
however, are clearly traceable in poems scattered over the eight volumes
of verse, and the totality is nothing less than an autobiographical chronicle of the very sort that Hardy, in more than one context and on more
than one occasion, denied his intention of writing.

What happened at this particular locale or at that specific moment of
time may best be identified by a reader who reorders the scattered
arrangement of the poems in a linear sequence, and who defines the
autobiographical elements in some such chronological sequence as
Pinion suggests. I do not want to paraphrase the content of these poems;
they are not particularly difficult reading experiences. What needs
closer attention, however, is the way in which Hardy dramatised his own
personality and the role that he played in the developing tragedy of his
marriage. For, although Emma is the major figure in these poems, the
elusive 'I' requires more attention than he usually receives, and the fact
that he has long since passed beyond the flush of erotic possibilities – the
fact that he can never be young again – is a significant element in the
establishment of tone. There is throughout the sequence a recognition of
the unbridgeable distance between the second decade of this century and
the memories, however vivid, of earlier and happier times.

The speaker of 'The Wind's Prophecy', for example, is disturbingly
aware that any love, however intensely held, is subject to change.[10] This
poem, dealing as it does with Hardy's 'first journey into Cornwall and the
drive from Launceston to St. Juliot (7 March 1870)', is clearly about two
women, one 'morosely gray', with 'ebon loops of hair', the resident of a
'city home', and the other with 'tresses flashing fair', living near the sea,
and not yet known. Emma's point of view, recorded in 'A Man Was
Drawing Near to Me', was imagined by Hardy on the basis of a passage in
Some Recollections, and 'The Wind's Prophecy' may be regarded as a matching poem. Emma is the woman toward whom the poet is moving,
across a dreary landscape, 'by barren farms', under 'a cloud that speaks of
wrecks', and near a headland, 'vulturine', that 'snores like old Skyrymer
in his sleep'. The atmosphere is disturbingly charged with omens and

foreboding; the poet moves from a romance that has failed to another that will fail; and though he commences by speaking of the woman whose arms he loves 'the best', he ends on a note of uncertainty: 'God grant she stay my own!' There is no question, moreover, but that the prophesying wind, responding to each of his outcries, is cheerlessly, fatalistically pointing to his future with Emma. The 'terrene' is wild and uninviting.

> From tides the lofty coastlands screen
> Come smitings like the slam of doors,
> Or hammerings on hollow floors,
> As the swell cleaves through caves unseen.

Whatever joy Hardy enjoyed with Emma may have largely diminished by the time he rewrote 'The Wind's Prophecy' from 'an old copy'.[11] When did he begin to brood about the transiency of the magic in his eyes, about the darkening of his 'radiance rare and fathomless', as expressed in 'When I Set Out from Lyonnesse'? In 'The Wind's Prophecy' the pre-monitions of unhappiness were recorded at an early stage.

The dots of ellipsis used as a device to link memories of the past, when Emma's beauties were most attractive, with the present realities of anticlimax and regret, are used in more than one poem. 'St. Launce's Revisited', which speaks of new tavern-holder and 'strange' tap-maid, yet hopes that the old faces might still greet him if he returned, concludes with acceptance of the inevitable awakening:

> Why waste thought,
> When I know them vanished
> Under earth; yea, banished
> Ever into nought!

The poet evokes 'love's old domain' ('At Castle Boterel') as a land he can never traverse again ('for my sand is sinking'), and perhaps his imaginings of the happy life Emma led at St Juliot could not withstand critical analysis of the reality; such seems to be the drift of the parenthetical expression 'In my thought has it seemed' in 'A Dream or No.' There is no denying the charm of Emma in image after image conjured up from depths of memory; but, also, the poet is unable to prevent a later sense of proportion and awareness from modifying his memories. Hardy recalls how concerned Emma was over the death of greenhouse plants because of an untended stove at St Juliot, and then he isolates himself from the fullness of her grief by measuring it:

> By the breakfast blaze
> Blank-faced spoke she,
> Her scared young look
> Seeming to be
> The very symbol
> Of tragedy.

The use of the word 'seeming' suggests a later perspective. If Emma's face expressed unhappiness at the condition of the plants she loved so well – frozen because they were 'cold, iced, forgot' – it was because her feeling of tragedy moved deeply within her, and not because she was attempting to impress her lover with how tragic she appeared. Any effort to calculate the sincerity of Emma's emotions – to judge them by aesthetic standards – affects the immediacy of these spots of time. And a reader may well attribute some of Hardy's most piteous lamentations for a past that cannot return to this unavoidable and regretted double perspective.

In 'At the Word "Farewell"' ' – a poem that Hardy, in *The Early Life*, thought might well have referred to 11 March 1870, when he said goodbye to Emma at the end of his first visit to Cornwall – he writes of 'a Plan of the past' that made the strengthening of his relationship to Emma a certainty. But he could not have known that at the time, particularly if (as has been speculated) he was still engaged to Tryphena Sparks; indeed, the conviction that the first meeting was a 'prelude' to a lifetime drama was not his, but Emma's. Hardy, in this poem, is remembering something about Emma's interpretation of their first meetings at St Juliot that he learned not at the time of those meetings, not even at the moment of parting ('I soon must be gone!'), but at a much later time.

Any love affair involves the beautification and idealisation of the love-object, and no man, nor woman either, will maintain forever the conviction that all is perfect on the other side. Still, it takes a while for the tracing of the stages to perfect love to become possible or desirable, and the mild but authentic humour of 'A Week', which delineates the maturing of Hardy's affection for Emma, is possible only because the events of the week are remembered after the event, i.e. after Sunday night has passed; and may even suggest that these reactions to Emma's personality were not reactions experienced during the first week of his visit to St Juliot. Were they, indeed, the reactions that he went through after he had returned to Dorchester?

> On Friday it was with a thrill
> In gazing towards your distant vill
> I owned you were my dear one still.

The past tense, betraying the passage of years rather than of days or hours, is significant also in 'Lines to a Movement in Mozart's E-Flat Symphony', for here Hardy is attempting to relive moments when his feelings for Emma were freshest and filled with 'rashness, ratheness, rareness, ripeness, richness.'

> Show me again the day
> When from the sandy bay
> We looked together upon the pestered sea! –

And this poem – one of the most serene in the canon, completely without the taint of regret that love had lured his life on to the impasse which late in the century he discovered could not be avoided – recreates (most readers will feel successfully) the happier incidents of the romance that led to 'the moment of that kiss'.

More characteristic is the ruefulness of the linked poems 'The Figure in the Scene' and 'Why Did I Sketch?' The poet remembers drawing Emma as a 'hooded' figure at Beeny Cliff, 'only her outline shown, / With rainfall marked across'. She has since died; and if the picture remains behind as 'a wordless irony', and if the poet can indulge himself in the conceit that even at this moment 'her rainy form is the Genius still of the spot, / Immutable, yea', he cannot entirely escape from a presentiment that the remembered vision may somehow be sinister. Knowing what he now knows, he would not sketch her form thus again:

> If you go drawing on down or cliff
> Let no soft curves intrude
> Of a woman's silhouette,
> But show the escarpments stark and stiff
> As in utter solitude;
> So shall you half forget.

Summer can never come again to Beeny Cliff, or for that matter anywhere ('It Never Looks Like Summer'), and perhaps the most searing regret of all, contained in 'Self-Unconscious', is that he would not have married Emma if, during the courtship, he could have seen his situation objectively.

> O it would have been good
> Could he then have stood
> At a clear-eyed distance, and conned the whole . . .

To what 'thing' does Hardy allude when, in this poem, he speaks of it as looming 'with an immortal mien'? It was looming *then*, when he was blindest and most in love, and when God might – Hardy writes 'should' – have shown him to himself 'as he was'. The process of growing up is one of continual readjustment to realities often 'too late to alter things', as Hardy, explicating a line in 'Self-Unconscious' to Vere H. Collins, commented with an ill-concealed regret. Learning what is best to do after the moment for effectively doing it has passed, then, constituted for Hardy 'the tragedy of youth'.

The 'I' he limns in poem after poem recognises the *shared* quality of the tragedy. The reasons why breathless romance turned into desperate and permanent alienation bridgeable only after death are only hinted at in these dramatic lyrics, but that Emma suffered no less than he did is never denied. In 'Near Lanivet, 1872', a poem that Hardy insisted was based on an event that had occurred before his marriage, Emma, dressed in white, takes up a pose at a crossways that 'made her look as one crucified'. 'If no one is bodily crucified now', she broods, 'In spirit one may be!' The personal statement contained in 'We Sat at the Window', which recounts an incident in Bournemouth, suggests that as early as 1875 both Hardy and Emma had run out of conversation and means of entertaining each other:

> Nothing to read, nothing to see
> Seemed in that room for her and me
> On Swithin's day.

He scarcely dared to speculate on the reasons why. The poem 'The Rift', seeking to identify the very moment when the hopelessness of regaining that first fine rapture became evident, when he first began to sink from his 'high sublime', admits that he never learned, and could never guess, his 'crime'. Did he pay too little attention to her needs, her loneliness? 'The Musical Box' suggests this as one part of the answer; but Hardy knew well how difficult, how impossible, it was to 'make the most of what is nigh', and the poem is more a tentative reflection than a clear statement of cause. Did he remove her from her natural setting, and cause the flower to wilt? Such is the message of 'Fetching Her', wherein Hardy speculates that Max Gate might have seemed 'an alien bower' to Emma; she always felt more at home in Cornwall than in Dorset. What, indeed, was the nature of 'that thwart thing' between them, 'which nothing cleaves or clears' ('The Division')? Was the problem explainable in terms of her 'inept' and offending remarks, her failure to judge well-meaning intentions and friends for their true worth ('You Were the Sort that Men Forget'); or to his own failure to appreciate her sterling qualities over and beyond his dismay at the problems created by her strong personality ('I Thought, My Heart')? He tried to distribute blame fairly between himself and Emma, and even, in several poems, to weight the scales in Emma's favour. 'The End of the Episode' warns us of the possibility that the truth of the relationship may be sicklied o'er with Hardy's self-pity:

> Ache deep; but make no moans:
> Smile out; but stilly suffer:
> The paths of love are rougher
> Than thoroughfares of stones.

'The Tolerance' and 'The Wound' emphasise, in their similar mood and tone, the possibility that Hardy took some masochistic pleasure in bearing up silently under the offences created by the rudeness of the beloved; in bearing his wound 'of which none knew'.

Yet it is a matter of emphasis, after all, and the miracle of the many poems written about his love affair with Emma is that the poet honestly admits that he can never arrive at a final decision as to who is more to blame. 'When Oats Were Reaped', presumably about a visit paid by Hardy to the cemetery of Stinsford church, where Emma lay buried, contains the poignant lines:

> I wounded one who's there, and now know well I wounded her;
> But, ah, she does not know that she wounded me!

Was he referring to what she had written in anger, to what he had read after her death? If so, the notable aspect of the admission is that he shares responsibility. He regrets not having accepted her attempt to reconcile their differences (and there may well have been more than the one mentioned in 'The Peace-Offering'). He did not pay sufficient attention to the songs she sang ('An Upbraiding'). He failed to express the badly wished-for appreciation of the music she played ('Penance'). He did not mind that, 'weak and lame', she could not accompany him on his walk 'to the hill-top tree' ('The Walk'). For that matter, on the last time she went in an automobile to pay a visit six miles away ('Your Last Drive') he was not with her; and he admits, with some chagrin, that if he had been, he would still not have seen in her face any anticipation of her death, less than a week later; the drift between them had progressed so far that he had become indifferent to her.

> I drove not with you . . . Yet had I sat
> At your side that eve I should not have seen
> That the countenance I was glancing at

Had a last-time look in the flickering sheen,
Nor have read the writing upon your face . . .

After Emma's death Hardy recognised the inevitability of the event, but
could not obliterate the memories of what had been or the possibilities
of different courses of action that, in the past, had existed at one moment
or another. But he was too much of a realist to sentimentalise the facts of
the case, and 'The Going' strikes almost a brutal note in its concluding
stanza:

Well, well! All's past amend,
Unchangeable. It must go.
I seem but a dead man held on end
To sink down soon . . .

The finality of these lines reminds us of the consistency of the persona
Hardy had created in the hundred-odd poems that have traced a complex
and darkening marriage relationship, a self-consciously ageing persona
about to leave the world for ever, as his beloved has already left it. He
does not look forward with pleasure to reunion with her, if indeed such
reunion is possible; they have known too much about each other, and
he has learned more about her after her death (he 'now' knows how
much he wounded her), for any uniting in the other world to be joyous;
often there is even a faint sinister note of dread in the mention of the
possibility. But he valued much about her. She loved the natural world:

Soon will be growing
Green blades from her mound,
And daisies be showing
Like stars on the ground,
Till she form part of them –
Ay – the sweet heart of them,
Loved beyond measure
With a child's pleasure
All her life round.

As an individual, she laughed, raced hillsides, confronted ocean spray.
As a social being, she appreciated parties and dinners, and enjoyed the
cut of fashionable clothes. As a helpmeet, she encouraged him to do
what lay closest to his heart when the financial prospects of authorship
looked shakiest. If she changed, he admitted to himself, it is in the nature
of human personality to change; one may not transfix character any
more than time itself. If he failed – and he admits more than once that he

did less than he might have, or the wrong thing altogether – he did so through his failure to appreciate her permanent need for emotional support.

His personality tends to be one of waiting watchfulness; only rarely does he act; only in a few poems is he a moving agent; more often he seems to be 'faltering forward' ('The Voice'). The miracle lies in the fact that they ever came together, and in several poems he speaks as if bemused by the opportunity to have secured her devotion for however brief a period it may have been. If he berates himself, it is for querulousness, for having sunk into a 'dun life', for having betrayed the hope of

> A very West-of-Wessex girl,
> As blithe as blithe could be,

that some day they might both visit Plymouth Hoe and 'study up and down / Its charms in company' ('The West-of-Wessex Girl'). It was a visit they never made together, though (in the final poem of Carl Weber's arrangement) he speaks of Emma as the woman who 'opened the door of the West', 'the door of Romance', 'the door of a Love', and 'the door of the Past' to him.

Hardy's love poems are full of ghosts, lost chances, and lingering regrets. They are cruelly afflicted by a sense of the power of Time, because locks of hair, painted miniatures, and even original 'air-blue' gowns can do no more than stir memories; because they are substitutes for what can never come again. Only a few lyrics sentimentalise the poet's youth by romancing about what might have happened if he or Emma had been other than what they in fact were. In 'The Clock of the Years', he is tempted by a Spirit to 'make the clock of the years go backward', so that he can view Emma 'as last before' him; 'then younger, younger she freshed'; but she 'waned child-fair', 'and smalled till she was nought at all', and finally became insignificant, 'as if / She had never been.'

> 'Better,' I plained,
> 'She were dead as before! The memory of her
> Had lived in me; but it cannot now!'
> And coldly his voice:
> 'It was your choice
> To mar the ordained.'

Still he went ahead and conjured from the past memories no less vivid because they were decades old. He relived ancient happinesses and bled again from ancient wounds. He defined his marriage as a failure, doomed by causes he only dimly understood, and into the nature of which he dared not, and knew he could not, inquire too searchingly; but he accepted his full share, and perhaps more than his share, of guilt and responsibility. And at the end, he saw himself as a creature who had given room in his life to 'loving, loss, despair':

> His head was white. His small form, fine aforetime,
>   Was shrunken with old age and battering wear.
> An eighty-years long plodder saw I pacing
>   Beside me there.
>
> ('The Seven Times')

If on occasion in reading these fine examples of a poet's craft, in sympathising with the reasons for the poet's love of 'an eyesome maiden', we forget Hardy's age at the time of composition of the overwhelming majority of these lyrics – his final fifteen years, a time of life when most men can revel in grandchildren and even great-grandchildren – we are eventually reminded, gently but inexorably, that Hardy's perspective is of an aged man. For ultimately these are poems of acceptance. The design is mysterious, the weaver unknown; but Hardy, acknowledging that in fact he cannot 'mar the ordained', allows us the privilege of sharing with him the story of his love for 'dearest Emmie'.

3
Attitudes to the Past

The concatenation of circumstances that led to the sinking of the *Titanic* on 15 April 1912 caused more than one historian of the time to feel uneasy over the inscrutable and unpredictable workings of Destiny; but only Hardy's famous poem, 'The Convergence of the Twain', prepared for the 'Dramatic and Operatic Matinée in Aid of the *Titanic* Disaster Fund' that was given at Covent Garden Theatre on 14 May, endures today as 'the one piece of imaginative literature occasioned by the *Titanic* that seems likely to survive all journalistic accounts and all fictional re-creations.'[1] As an occasional poem, it might well be treated in another chapter. But as a grimly hostile reflection on attitudes current in the twentieth century, on modern *hubris*, the poem formulates a position of some concern to our understanding of Hardy's perspective on the past, which increasingly affected both the number and content of the poems contained in his final volumes of verse.

The poem is too well known to require paraphrase or explication. Its argument, that the iceberg and the great passenger liner had been predestined to meet, is expectably deterministic, and 'the Spinner of the Years' is simply another name for the Immanent Will. But Hardy's emphasis fell on the 'vaingloriousness' of the ship that J. Bruce Ismay had commissioned, Thomas Andrews had helped to build, and E. J. Smith had captained. The rendezvous – 'the intimate welding of their later history' – had become inevitable once 'the Pride of Life that planned her' set out to build the unsinkable ship. Hardy, in brief, was deeply disturbed by the 'human vanity' that so easily had assumed its ability to direct events, so unthinkingly had placed mirrors 'to glass the opulent'. At the bottom of the ocean – two miles down – the 'salamandrine fires' were stilled, the 'gilded gear' seemed out of place, and

> Jewels in joy designed
> To ravish the sensuous mind
> Lie lightless, all their sparkles bleared and black and blind.

He was, no doubt, expressing a sermon against *vanitas vanitatum* no more than did the Bishop of Winchester, who called the *Titanic* 'a monument and warning to human presumption'; or Joseph Conrad, who bitterly referred to the ship as 'a sort of marine Ritz, proclaimed unsinkable, and sent adrift with its casual population upon the sea, without enough boats, without enough seamen (but with a Parisian café, and four hundreds of poor devils of waiters)'; or Henry Adams, who saw the disaster as a blow struck 'at confidence in our mechanical success'. As Adams wrote to a friend, 'By my blessed Virgin, it is awful!'

Inevitably, among the 1513 men, women, and children of the 2224 aboard who perished when the ship, 'so gaily great', up-ended and died, at least one personal friend – W. T. Stead, editor of the *Review of Reviews* – was lost. (Hardy referred to the loss of 'two acquaintances'.) As much might have been expected, since Hardy had long since become accustomed to move in distinguished social circles, and the casualties included the wealthy as well as the anonymous of both Great Britain and the United States. But the sense of *personal* loss is not an element in Hardy's poem, nor does 'The Convergence of the Twain' have anything to offer in the way of lamentation for the victims, even taken as a collective whole. The poem is, rather, a statement of philosophy buried in the form of an attack upon contemporary arrogance. The modern world, like some 'smart ship' increasing every moment 'in stature, grace, and hue', sails on to meet, ultimately, its Nemesis.

We understand very well the tartness of the message, and in several contexts Hardy has much else to say about the tastelessness or vulgarity of this century. His unwillingness to concede much in the way of literary merit to the modern theatre is a continuing motif; his decision to abjure novel-writing is correctly referred to as a commentary on the condition of developing trends in modern literature; and the 'Apology' to *Late Lyrics and Earlier* (1922) makes a dour allusion to 'these disordered years of our prematurely afflicted century'. And these are only the references of an artist to his profession; more evidence may be amassed to show that Hardy disliked a great deal about politicians and political events, social trends, and various events reported in the press. As he wrote to Florence Henniker on 5 June 1919 (a time when many others were speculating hopefully about the shape of things to come), 'I should care more for my birthdays if at each succeeding one I could see any sign of real improvement in the world – as at one time I fondly hoped there was; but I fear that what appears much more evident is that it is getting worse and worse. All development is of a material and scientific kind – and scarcely any addition to our knowledge is applied to objects philanthropic or ameliorative. I almost think that people were less pitiless towards their fellow-creatures – human and animal – under the Roman Empire than they are now. . . .'[2]

But Hardy's conservatism in any number of responses to inquiries about questions of the day posted by journalists and friends is not necessarily testimony to his desire to resurrect the conditions of his childhood; in F. Scott Fitzgerald's fine phrase, to 'beat on, boats against the current, borne back ceaselessly into the past'. Indeed, Hardy's relationship to the 1840s and 1850s is by no means a simple matter, and a great deal of nonsense has been written about the 'singing in the heather' (Edmund Gosse's phrase) that presumably went on in his earlier novels. Closer inspection of those fictions shows very little interest in sentimentalising the drudgery, poverty, and meanness of the Dorset countryside. Any review of the historical matrix would confirm one critic's judgement that Casterbridge was unlike the small towns of Mrs Gaskell and George Eliot, i.e. it was never simply a place 'with an essentially healthy though somewhat narrow and limited code.'[3] Why this stereotype of a 'stable and cheerful Old England' should so distort appreciation of Hardy's work even today, after the generations of research that followed the appearance of Hardy's 'The Dorsetshire Labourer' (1883), Joseph Arch's *Life* (1898), and Henry Rider Haggard's *Rural England* (1902), is unclear; but Hardy would have been dismayed to learn – had he lived that long – the persistence of gross misreadings of his relationship to the past. Relatively recent, and in many other ways intelligent and sensitive, readers of Hardy's work continue to distort the relationship.

Donald Davie, in a stimulating (though hyperbolic) survey of Hardy's influence on modern British poetry, defines an anthology piece as a 'poem which, whether by luck or design, and whatever its other virtues, cannot give offence'.[4] He cites as two examples of what he has in mind 'The Darkling Thrush' and 'The Oxen'. The implications of this position – that Hardy shied away from the writing of a serious poem which would have something to say that might inevitably offend this or that fraction of the reading public – are disturbing to contemplate; Davie does not mend matters by referring to 'the dishonesties, or the opportunities for dishonesty, which attend a poet who, like Hardy, declares that his highest ambition is to place one or two poems in an anthology like *The Golden Treasury*'. The argument, borrowed in part from R. P. Blackmur's essay, 'The Shorter Poems of Thomas Hardy' (*Southern Review*, summer), 1940 conceives of Hardy as an 'expert technician, imperious within his expertise, diffident or indifferent outside it'; and it naggingly raises again the old question of whether poetry unconcerned with 'major issues of national policy' can ever hope to be 'great' in Davie's and Blackmur's sense of the term.

One cannot argue successfully on these grounds. There is no way to maintain convincingly the position that Hardy, a private poet, is writing successful and often great poems when the prime criterion of merit is a poet's willingness to embark on themes of public concern. If one agrees with Davie that Hardy's 'engaging modesty and his decent liberalism' are insufficiently radical, fail to go to the roots as a poet should and must (it is his 'duty'), then those who frame the conditions of the debate will insist that Hardy has sold short 'the poetic vocation, for himself and his successors' (p. 41). From the narrowness of this view, however generous other aspects of Davie's tribute may be, there can be no appeal.

Nevertheless, Hardy seems to be saying something about the past in his poetry that deserves closer inspection, and perhaps we need do no more than concede, without regret, the unusualness of 'The Convergence of the Twain' as a public topical statement, as a denunciation of important aspects of the twentieth century. Hardy did not write many such poems. His art is more often tinctured by regrets; it impresses us as being personal but indirect.

'The Oxen', no whit the worse because it is an anthology poem, contrasts the tribal wisdom of the 'elder' – who once assured his youthful audience that oxen kneel at midnight on Christmas Eve – with the febrile wisdom of the poet's persona, who, come of age, recognises the impossibility of believing any longer in 'so fair a fancy'. But if anyone were to invite him as a grown man to visit 'the lonely barton by yonder coomb' to see the kneeling oxen, he knows that he would

> go with him in the gloom,
> Hoping it might be so.

There is no certainty that what he believed as a child was true then, or can be demonstrated to be true now; 'hoping' is the operative word. But equally important is the innocence of the belief itself, whether or not it corresponds to reality. What the elder has said, his audience has believed:

> Nor did it occur to one of us there
> To doubt they were kneeling then.

Nor does the child come to manhood blame the elder for having mythologised. He remembers, rather, that he sat listening to the elder as a member of 'a flock', and that he rested 'by the embers in hearthside ease'. No facile conclusion that the past is a better place may be drawn from

Hardy's deliberate contrast between time-periods; but faith came more easily then.

Hardy's poems about the past are fragments shored against his ruin, and he admitted that for him the past was irrecoverable. On many occasions, not the least being that memorable date of 16 November 1910 when he was presented with 'the freedom of Dorchester', he viewed with alarm the rebuildings and the 'reconstructions' that had defaced his native town. 'Old All-Saints was, I believe', he said dryly, 'demolished because its buttresses projected too far into the pavement. What a reason for destroying a record of 500 years in stone! I knew the architect who did it; a milder-mannered man never scuttled a sacred edifice.'[5] He went on to say that such depredations could only be prevented by 'the education of their owners or temporary trustees, or, in the case of churches, by Government guardianship', and, in a sombre mood, reflected:

And when all has been said on the desirability of preserving as much as can be preserved, our power to preserve is largely an illusion. Where is the Dorchester of my early recollection – I mean the human Dorchester – the kernel – of which the houses were but the shell? Of the shops as I first recall them not a single owner remains; only in two or three instances does even the name remain. As a German author has said, 'Nothing is permanent but change.'

The mildness of tone is memorable, for, even as he speculated that the future of Dorchester would not resemble its past ('we may be sure of that'), he accepted what he, more than many of his contemporaries, saw as inevitable. 'Like other provincial towns', he concluded, 'it will lose its individuality – has lost much of it already. We have become almost a London suburb owing to the quickened locomotion, and, though some of us may regret this, it has to be.'

There are, in fact, three large categories for these poems: his reflections on history as such (often the relationship of Roman artifacts to life in modern England), on Dorset at mid-century, and on the significance of his own childhood experiences as seen through the isinglass of time. So far as the first category is concerned, Hardy had ample reason to think of Casterbridge as an ancient town; the earthworks at Maiden Castle and Poundbury (Pommery) were palpable presences; they served as important locales in his fictions.

Casterbridge announced old Rome in every street, alley, and precinct. It looked Roman, bespoke the art of Rome, concealed dead men of Rome. It was impossible to dig more than a foot or two

deep about the town fields and gardens without coming upon
some tall soldier or other of the Empire, who had lain there in his
silent unobtrusive rest for a space of fifteen hundred years. . . . [6]

Hardy became sufficiently excited over discoveries of Roman graves made
during the excavations for Max Gate – only three hundred yards from
a 'fine and commanding tumulus called Conquer Barrow' – to prepare an
address (May 1884) to the members of the Dorset Natural History and
Antiquarian Field Club, a society that had been founded in 1875.[7] He
referred, with cautious respect, to 'the presumably great Romano-
British cemetery upon Fordington Hill', and concluded his talk with a
speculation on what 'the living Durnovaria of fourteen or fifteen hundred years ago' might have looked like to an observer who stood on any
commanding point of elevated ground:

> . . . where stood the large buildings, were they small, how did the
> roofs group themselves, what were the gardens like, if any, what
> social character had the streets, what were the customary noises,
> what sort of exterior was exhibited by these hybrid Romano-
> British people, apart from the soldiery?

Hardy contributed his talents and time to the Club – which he had
joined while living at Wimborne in the early 1880s – in others ways; it was
difficult to be indifferent; after all, Henry Moule had organised the
County Museum. 'A Tryst at an Ancient Earthwork' (first published in
March 1885) reflects Hardy's interest in the sombre fortress of Mai-Dun,
and A Group of Noble Dames (1891) fictionally limns several of the members
of the Field Club and their antiquarian interests.

'The Roman Gravemounds' – its occasion the burial of a favourite cat
– is, in its essence, a poem about the impossibility of escaping the weight
of memories. The chief figure of the poem confesses that he has no
knowledge of the 'fames' and the 'achievements' of those who, almost
two millennia earlier, had walked the earth near Max Gate. He is less
interested in the 'Empire long decayed' than in the 'little white furred
thing, stiff of limb', of importance to nobody save her mourner, that he is
bringing to a final resting-place. Perhaps, as the poem concludes, the
mourner's mood has a charm for the poet, and the 'sages of history' will
inevitably memorialise 'Rome's long rule' anyhow, while the pet needs
at least one elegiac remembrance:

> The furred thing is all to him – nothing Rome!

But Rome is all around him; the cat will be buried 'by Rome's dim relics'; and the vastness of Rome in its original splendour can never be forgotten.

> 'Vast was Rome,' he must muse, 'in the world's regard,
> Vast it looms there still, vast it ever will be. . . .'

'The Shadow on the Stone', written several years later, encapsulates Hardy's reverent – and even superstitious – attitude toward a five-foot stone, surrounded by 'ashes and half charred bones', that had been unearthed at Max Gate. Was it a Druid altar – a place to which Emma returned years after her death? The poet does not want to look behind him lest his 'dream should fade', but he knows that 'the shifting shadows' on the 'Druid stone that broods in the garden white and lone' may well hide a shape, an apparition. There are memories in the garden, memories not wholly of Emma either.

In the second category, Dorset at mid-century, Hardy conjures a world now forever gone:

> We two kept house, the Past and I,
> The Past and I;
> Through all my tasks it hovered nigh
> leaving me never alone . . .
>
> ('The Ghost of the Past')

The number of such poems is limited, but they breathe nostalgia for persons and places Hardy had no way of knowing well first-hand. For example, 'Transformations' imagines that a yew may be, in part, a man his grandsire knew; that a branch of the yew

> may be his wife,
> A ruddy human life
> Now turned to a green shoot. . . .

The continuity of life – human beings become 'grasses', they do not remain permanently underground, they enter into the 'growths of upper air' – is a continuing element in Hardy's thinking. Immortality, as Hardy believed, is the continuation of memory.

Yet by far the largest number of lyrics (the third category) deal with Hardy's reminiscences of his own youth, and only a few of them record the self-satisfaction of 'A Private Man on Public Men' (one of the final poems of *Winter Words*). 'Self-satisfaction' may not be the proper word even here to describe the assessment of Hardy's life, spent far from the turmoil of London,

> Tasting years of moderate gladness
> Mellowed by sundry days of sadness,

though the choice of privacy at the expense of opportunities to achieve business or political success had been deliberately made. More frequently these poems offer tantalising and rueful glimpses of what life for young Tom must have been like. They form an extraordinary grouping. In *Satires of Circumstance* they include 'In Front of the Landscape' and 'Seventy-four and Twenty'. *Moments of Vision* offers 'Apostrophe to an Old Psalm Tune', 'Heredity', 'Quid Hic Agis?', 'To My Father's Violin', ' "In the Seventies" ', 'The Pedigree', 'Life Laughs Onward', 'Transformation', 'Great Things', 'Old Furniture', 'The Ageing House', 'He Fears his Good Fortune', 'He Revisits his First School', and ' "For Life I had Never Cared Greatly" '. In *Late Lyrics and Earlier* a reader searching for clues to how Hardy thought of the 1840s and 1850s will want to examine carefully 'At the Entering of the New Year', 'In the Small House', 'On One who Lived and Died where he was Born', ' "I was the Midmost" ', and the often-anthologised 'An Ancient to Ancients'. In *Human Shows, Far Phantasies, Songs, and Trifles* two poems are relevant to this consideration: 'Shortening Days at the Homestead' and 'Song to an Old Burden'. And in *Winter Words in Various Moods and Metres* Hardy speaks of his growing-up in 'Concerning his Old Home', 'Childhood among the Ferns', 'So Various', 'A Self-Glamourer', ' "We Say We Shall Not Meet" ', 'He Never Expected Much', 'I Looked Back', and 'Not Known', as well as 'A Private Man on Public Men'. Taken together, these poems offer a rich and consistent portrait – far from pessimistic in tone, but not wholly innocent in its pleasures recollected in tranquillity either, save in a few poems like 'Shortening Days at the Homestead'.

Growing old is a process one puts up with. Hardy, even at an age perhaps no greater than that of Housman's melancholy Shropshire lad, seems to have been rueful rather than angry or bitter. Missed opportunities seem less important than the simple recognition of the impossibility of change: the Ancient is what he is because he has survived. He does not claim superior wisdom or virtue. He rides no thesis. He recognises the claim of youth – the 'red-lipped and smooth-browed' – to have their turn:

> These younger press; we feel our rout
> Is imminent to Aïdes' den. . . .
>
> ('An Ancient to Ancients')

There may have been marvellous dances, sports, paintings, novels in the

Victorian years, and they may even have been better than today's art, but such is not the thrust of the Ancient's peroration. Rather, even as he yields to the newer generation, he places a proper and dignified valuation on what his fellow-Ancients have accomplished, while frankly admitting that tomorrow may bring in its own equally valid pleasures.

> Much is there waits you we have missed;
> Much lore we leave you worth the knowing,
> Much, much has lain outside our ken:
> Nay, rush not: time serves: we are going,
>   Gentlemen.

The candour of 'Much, much has lain outside our ken' is disarming, because here (and elsewhere) the claim of the poet is neither more nor less than this: if one lives long enough, one learns how to maintain a delicate equilibrium with biological, historical, and temporal forces.

'Biological forces' – as a phrase – refers to Hardy's health. The poet's illnesses – though never again as debilitating as the internal bleeding which made the writing of A Laodicean (1880–81) so agonising – were sufficiently numerous to justify the fear of many of Hardy's friends that such a fragile creature could not live to his full threescore and ten. A popular misreading of 'The Darkling Thrush' (written even before its appended date of '31st December 1900') identifies Hardy himself with the 'aged thrush, frail, gaunt, and small, / In blast-beruffled plume'; it was almost an immediate misunderstanding among Hardy's contemporaries. Hardy's letters and autobiography during these years are filled with allusions to such matters as leg pains caused by bicycling, influenza caused by the damp weather of London, more influenza in Dorchester, colds of varying degrees of unpleasantness and intensity, weak eyesight, 'a violent bronchitis and racking cough', 'a violent cough and cold', a bad throat, the return of 'an old complaint – internal inflammation – which, though not violent, has been extremely tedious', etc. Husbanding his strength for major occasions, he often found it too taxing to wait up for the ringing in of a new year.

It would, of course, be unusual for any man to proceed unachingly to the age of eighty-eight, yet Hardy from a very early age was conscious of how precarious was his grip on Life. Even the surgeon who delivered him into the world had thrown him aside as dead, and only 'the estimable woman who attended as monthly nurse' had rescued him with the cry, 'Dead! Stop a minute: he's alive enough, sure!' If she had not done so (according to a family tradition which Hardy believed), 'he might never have walked the earth.'[8] Hardy's complaints about ill health were closely related to his abiding sense of mortality. His diary records one poignant entry under the date of 12 October 1892:

> Hurt my tooth at breakfast-time. I look in the glass. Am conscious of the humiliating sorriness of my earthly tabernacle, and of the sad fact that the best of parents could do no better for me. . . . Why should a man's mind have been thrown into such close, sad, sensational, inexplicable relations with such a precarious object as his own body![9]

Hence the otherwise preternatural multiplicity of references to the body: the 'family face' whose 'flesh perishes' but which lives on nevertheless ('Heredity'); 'hands behind hands, growing paler and paler' as the generations pass ('Old Furniture'); the not unexpected analogy between 'mouldy green' walls and an aged head ('The Ageing House'); the self-awareness of how he looks ('an aspect of hollow-eyed care') as 'He Revisits his First School'; the extended description of the poet as 'a frail aged figure . . . / All gone his life's prime, / All vanished his vigour, / And fine, forceful frame' ('On One who Lived and Died where he was Born'); the cheeks that 'have wanned to whiteness' ('Songs to an Old Burden'). The earthly tabernacle is apt at any unexpected moment to shiver and collapse into primal clay.

Hardy's view of the nature of history, as might be expected, had largely been shaped by the time he was writing the concluding scenes of *The Dynasts*. He was, after all, an admirer of Tolstoy as a large-hearted and ethically admirable human being; he owned a four-volume set of Nathan H. Dole's translation of *War and Peace*, which he marked at passages apposite to moments in Napoleon's career that he intended to dramatise; and he seemed to have been particularly struck by Tolstoy's denial of the freedom of the will. But in the final three decades of his life he saw himself as a chronicler of memories that might otherwise go unrecorded. Stonehenge – to which he returned again and again, as if, like Tess, he saw the final working-out of his destiny there – was most appropriately viewed 'at twilight'[10] as 'the wonder of Salisbury Plain, and of England, which it has been for so many centuries – a sacred possession.'[11] The poignant 'Lausanne: In Gibbon's Old Garden: 11–12 P.M.' commemorates a visit to the Hôtel Gibbon, where Hardy maintained a nocturnal vigil on the night of 27 June 1897, on the very spot where Gibbon, one hundred years earlier, had mused after writing 'the last lines of the last page' of his monumental history of the Roman Empire; though Hardy, late in life, could not recall whether the coincidence of dates was accidental, there is no question that he saw significant correspondences between

Gibbon's insistence on the historical truth and his own concept of the need for 'Candour in English Fiction'. Gibbon, like Hardy himself, had understood the full meaning of 'sage Milton's wormwood words':

> '*Truth like a bastard comes into the world*
> *Never without ill-fame to him who gives her birth.*'

He loved 'the reposefulness and peace' of cathedrals, and once, in his diary, wrote that 'the Close of Salisbury, under the full summer moon on a windless midnight, is as beautiful a scene as any I know in England – or for the matter of that elsewhere.'[12] He found it hard to stop thinking about Napoleon even after he no longer wanted to write about him. Once, in response to a gift of Raymond Guyot's *Napoleon* from Mr and Mrs Granville-Barker, he spoke of the man 'who finished the Revolution with "a whiff of grapeshot", and so crushed not only its final horrors but all the worthy aspirations of its earlier time, made them as if they had never been, and threw back human altruism scores, perhaps hundreds of years.'[13] On another occasion, reading a letter sent by a Dorset man from Berlin in June 1815, Hardy mused on the correspondent's explanation of the cause of German militarism: Napoleon. 'It would be strange', Hardy wrote to General J. H. Morgan, who had been trying to check on factual details recorded in *The Dynasts*, 'to find that Napoleon was really the prime cause of German militarism! What a Nemesis for the French nation!'[14] And to identify Hardy's enlightened antiquarianism, his zest for the continuity of tradition despite the passage of centuries, we need only point to his numerous public statements on the linkages in the history of Dorchester and its environs; as, for example, his retracing of the ownerships of the village of Bockhampton from the Norman Conquest to the beginning of the nineteenth century, in a speech given to mark the opening of the Bockhampton Reading-room and Club (2 December 1919).

Familiarity with the small did not mean that Hardy saw himself, or mankind in general, exercising control over the large. The sweep of historical forces was inexorable. Some questions, he decided well before the 1890s (when he recorded the thought), 'are made unimportant by their very magnitude. For example, the question whether we are moving in Space this way or that; the existence of a God, etc.'[15] He believed that he himself was an irrationalist, his own views being 'mere impressions that frequently change'.[16] He saw similarities between his philosophy and that of Spinoza and Einstein: 'that neither Chance nor Purpose governs the universe, but Necessity.'[17]

Yet even if the ancients had not been able to direct their own destinies, they were able to find consolation in their gods and heroes. Hardy was convinced that the right to be modern was purchased at enormous cost: such consolation was no longer available. He quoted sympathetically Leslie Stephen's lament, 'The old ideals have become obsolete, and the new are not yet constructed.'[18] The modern world, choking on the materialistic benefits provided by Science, had not gone forward morally.[19] In 1920, sceptical about the powers of 'the young and feeble League of Nations', he wrote:

> People are not more humane, so far as I can see, than they were in the year of my birth. Disinterested kindness is less. The spontaneous good will that used to characterize manual workers seems to have departed. One day of late a railway porter said to a feeble old lady, a friend of ours, 'See to your luggage yourself.' Human nature had not sunk so low as that in 1840.[20]

It was hardly a meliorist speaking, after all his protestations against the charge of 'Pessimist', in the response Hardy made to Dr Max Dessoir at the University of Berlin, who had asked – before the Great War – for some comments on the culture and thought of the time:

> We call our age an age of Freedom. Yet Freedom, under her incubus of armaments, territorial ambitions smugly disguised as patriotism, superstitions, conventions of every sort, is of such stunted proportions in this her so-called time, that the human race is likely to be extinct before Freedom arrives at maturity.[21]

Equal justice for all, no less for Hardy than for international organisations, was the goal; the Golden Rule for the 'inferior' races as well as for the English (Hardy detested the word 'British', which he called a 'vague, unhistoric and pinchbeck title'); a recognition of the fact (in Hardy's mind it was a fact) that 'the common origin of all species is ethical.'[22] But the goal would not be attained in this century, nor for many centuries to come, if ever. As he wrote glumly in one of his 'Birthday notes' (2 June 1920): 'Nature's indifference to the advance of her species along what we are accustomed to call civilized lines makes the late war of no importance to her, except as a sort of geological fault in her continuity.'[23]

Now how does a human being given to such speculations sustain faith in creative work if indeed he believes that yesterday must not be sentimentalised, and suspects that the historical forces operant today may have tarnished the nobler and more altruistic sentiments of the past? Writing to a Dr C. W. Saleeby about Bergson's philosophy (probably early in 1915), Hardy confessed to one technique for minimising the

1 Thomas Hardy, a sketch by William Rothenstein, 1915

2a Emma Lavinia Hardy in her later years

2b Hardy at the turn of the century

3a Max Gate when first built, showing Conquer Barrow

3b The garden at Max Gate

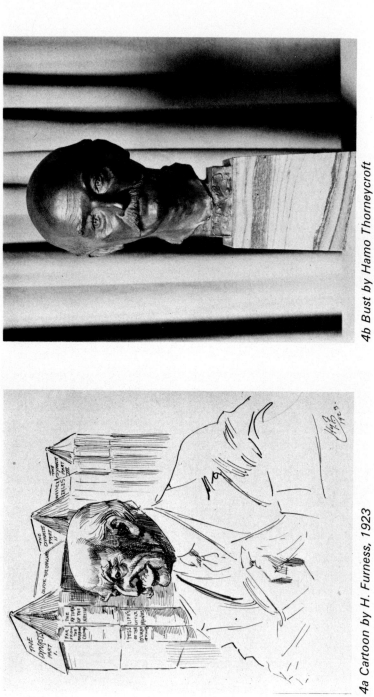

4b Bust by Hamo Thorneycroft

4a Cartoon by H. Furness, 1923

5b Poster for the Kingsway Theatre production of
The Dynasts

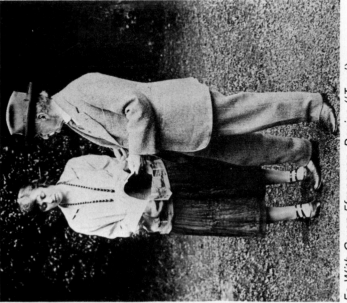

5a With Gwen Ffrangcon-Davies ('Tess')

6 Hardy and Florence on their way to vote

7 With Edmund Gosse at Max Gate, 1927

8 The Prince of Wales' visit, 1923

horrors of his contemporary world: 'Half my time – particularly when writing verse – I "believe" (in the modern sense of the word) not only in the things Bergson believes in, but in spectres, mysterious voices, intuitions, omens, dreams, haunted places, etc., etc. But I do not believe in them in the old sense of the word any more for that. . . .'[24] In brief, he exploited for literary and imaginative purposes the Gothic and supernatural elements that earlier generations had accepted as having a reality of their own, and he confessed, perhaps a little wryly, that he could not wholly disbelieve them himself.

Moreover, the bleakness of these opinions about the inability of the human race to awake from the nightmare that is history was recorded in far fewer poems than one might assume. Hardy quite rightly resented the efforts of reviewers to generalise about his opinions on the basis of a few poems taken out of the context of surrounding poems; his cheerless poems about the developments of history were by no means as numerous as hastily-judging critics – and even friends like Alfred Noyes – claimed they were; and some of his sensitivity, even when he had gone well beyond a time of life where such charges should have mattered, was surely related to a lifelong unwillingness to be labelled an atheist.

Even so, the 'ageing poems' (no satisfactory title for them exists) are gentler than this quick review of Hardy's personal opinions might have led us to expect; they neither rage against the dying of the light nor intimate in any way that after the poet's death will come the deluge. Still another reason for drawing a careful distinction between what he personally held as credo and what he put into these poems is our remembrance of that tough-cored idealism expressed in – for example – his impatience at William James's pragmatic notion that Truth is what will work. 'A worse corruption of language', he wrote angrily in his notebook (approximately July 1925), 'was never perpetrated.'[25] He was very sensitive to temporal forces operating in the twentieth century; though wary of the possibility of being misunderstood, he sought to clarify – again and again – his point of view toward issues of concern to Englishmen. This is the Hardy who, in addition to receiving honours (the Order of Merit and the freedom of Dorchester in 1910, the gold medal of the Royal Society of Literature in 1912, the honorary degree of Litt.D. from Cambridge University and an Honorary Fellowship of Queen's College, Oxford, as well as honorary degrees from the Universities of Aberdeen, St Andrews and Bristol), served society in general and his fellow Casterbridgians in particular as a prime mover in the Dorset Natural History and Antiquarian Field Club, as Governor of Dorchester Grammar School (1909–25), as President of the Society of Authors (1909, taking over from George Meredith), and as a Grand Juror at the Assizes asked to judge food-profiteering cases at the Police Courts (during the Great War). He believed in the capabilities of the human race to endure, but only fitfully in its chances of prevailing. Looking past the easy opportunities to indulge in nay-saying, he denounced 'patriotism' because it was an obstacle to world peace, which he continually preached was worth striving for. In April 1923, writing to John Galsworthy, he expressed the opinion that

> the exchange of international thought is the only possible salvation for the world: and I was decidedly premature when I wrote at the beginning of the South African War that I hoped to see patriotism not confined to realms, but circling the earth, I still maintain that such sentiments ought to prevail.[26]

(He could not refrain from adding, 'Whether they will do so before the year 10,000 is of course what sceptics may doubt.') He said of himself that he passionately hated 'injustice and barbarity' (in connection with the poem 'Compassion', written in June 1924), and it was true. His support of capital punishment – expressed in a letter to a writer of a report on the subject at Stanford University (1903) – was characteristically argued on the ground that it 'operates as a deterrent from deliberate crimes against life to an extent that no other form of punishment can rival.'[27] (He did not want to discuss 'the question of the moral right of a community to inflict that punishment'.)

Hardy's fascination with Jesus ('a young reformer who, though only in the humblest walk of life, became the most famous personage the world has ever known') explains, at least partially, his support of a Jewish state in Palestine a full decade before the outbreak of the First World War. Though he foresaw difficulties that might recommend the strategy of building up a Jewish colony first 'in, say, East Africa' before making a bid for Palestine 'as a sort of annexe', he approved what then seemed to be an impossible dream; the Jews were a people of 'extraordinary character and history' who deserved no less. If he were a Jew himself, as he wrote to Israel Zangwill, 'I should be a rabid Zionist no doubt.'[28]

Most often in his thoughts was the condition of modern literature. Criticism was in a parlous state; as Hardy said to W. M. Parker, a distinguished editor of the letters and journals of Sir Walter Scott, no contemporary critic, operating on the basis of a 'quick critical insight for what is of permanent literary value', was writing in either England or America.[29] In addition, critical journals were continually seeking to establish the degree of popularity of a work of fiction rather than to define its intrinsic merits. He expressed dismay that the newly-founded *Canadian Bookman* advertised 'The Best Sellers', and he wrote, with some asperity, 'Of all marks of the *un*-literary journal this is the clearest.'[30] In such a climate, meritorious fiction had difficulty in prospering. The values that Hardy attributed to Anatole France – who came to London for an honorary dinner (December 1913) that Hardy unfortunately could not attend – were values that he found lacking in younger novelists and poets: 'the value of organic form and symmetry, the force of reserve, and the emphasis of understatement.'[31] Writing under the influence of Arnold Bennett, they were contemptuous of plot, they had no feeling for romance: 'Romance must always be an essential element, no matter how many other qualities it contain, in a novel addressed to a wide novel-reading public.'[32]

He disapproved of the 'Georgian Poets' (their use of the soubriquet confused the poetic chronology, lacked the modesty of true genius, etc.); snorted that Yeats did not know what he believed; disliked obscurity and quoted approvingly Spencer's remark that 'the energy devoted to finding out the meaning of what one reads is spent at the cost of what might have been given to appreciating it'; censured endless rewriting and tinkering with texts, which spoiled 'freshness and spontaneity'; told Vere H. Collins in a tone that brooked no argument, 'Miss Mew is far and away the best living woman poet – who will be read when others are forgotten',[33] but the judgement may have been a commentary on the quality of poetesses included in J. C. Squire's *Book of Women's Verse* (Miss Mew had been omitted); and even as he gave qualified approval to Blunden's efforts ('You know he's quite a boy – a sort of Shelley, and he does the sort of things Shelley would have done'), he admitted that his personal liking for a writer might affect his judgement of particular poems. Modern literature was assuming 'a structureless and conglomerate character', modern criticism was stultified by '*the unwilling mind*', he had been personally abused too often to forgive. When he visited Oxford to attend a performance of *The Dynasts* by the Oxford University Dramatic Society (1920), Charles Morgan was both surprised and distressed to hear Hardy inveigh against critics: 'Such a belief indicated the only failure of balance, the only refusal to seek the truth, which I perceived in Hardy, and I was glad when the coming of a visitor, who was, I think, secretary of the Society of Dorset Men, led him away from criticism to plainer subjects.'[34] Hardy was not to change his mind; one of the very last entries in his second notebook (16 October 1926) recorded a definition of critics as dreary people who 'fix the rank of their author by his value as an artificer, not as an inventor; a shaper, not as a creator. Critics of plays likewise.'[35] Toward the end of the Great War – when, all things considered, the English had more stupendous problems to consider than the value, or lack of value, of modern poetry – Hardy could not resist a disappointed – if humorous – comment on 'the neglect of poetry by the modern English': 'The poet is like one who enters and mounts a platform to give an address as announced. He opens his page, looks around, and finds the hall – *empty*.'[36]

This recapitulation of opinions held on personal health, the currents of history, and the coloration of the modern world should be seen as a necessary prelude to judging the whole matter of Hardy's interest in idealising the Dorset of his childhood. For the poems, by themselves, do not tell us enough; they are evidence, but not the whole truth; though Hardy felt obliged to admit on his eighty-sixth birthday that the world had never promised him more than 'neutral-tinted haps and such', had never promised him that life would be fair, had indeed kept faith with him ('He Never Expected Much'), he sometimes softened or evaded in his poems the more depressing aspects of what he knew. A reader might never gather from the last five volumes of verse, for example, that the improved material comforts of an agricultural labourer's life had been acquired at the high cost of what Hardy, in an important letter to Rider Haggard (March 1902), called 'village tradition – a vast mass of unwritten folk-lore, local chronicle, local topography, and nomenclature.'[37] And Hardy did not have a final opinion, was perhaps reluctant to make up his mind, to dramatize the questions in his poetry that his awareness of local history kept bringing before his consciousness. When he was young, 'workfolk' stayed where they were because – as Hardy finally learned – 'they had neither the means nor the knowledge in old times that they have now.' Their instability of tenure, their rights to no more than life-hold, their poverty, their hunger, their vulnerability to insult and rejection at annal hiring-fairs, in brief, their painful dependence on greedy farmers who paid no heed to national interest or simple human decency, guaranteed the mass migration to cities as soon as the opportunity presented itself. The streets of the city were not paved with gold, of course, and many who left Dorset wound up in the slums of London. Those who stayed behind benefited (understandably) because scarcity of labour meant that their work was valued, and paid for, at a higher rate; but Hardy saw quite clearly that the process of cultural impoverishment was accelerating in Dorsetshire villages that were declining slowly but steadily after 1841, or else were reaching a peak in 1851 or 1871 and declining after that. The villages were not depopulated, as the relevant statistics show, but the dwindling, the stagnancy, must be set against the fact that England's population, during the decades of Queen Victoria's reign, experienced tremendous growth.[38]

As a consequence, the poems of nostalgia should be read carefully; the past is permanently the past, and it is wholly unshaded in only a few poems like 'Great Things' and 'Shortening Days at the Homestead', or resolutely optimistic in an atypical poem like 'For Life I Had Never Cared Greatly'. Edmund Gosse was wrong to claim that Hardy's rural gods, at any stage of his career, even the earliest, were 'all homely and benign'. Hardy loved the memories of fancy-fiddling for a wedding ('Figures of jigging fieldfolk – / Saviours of corn and hay' in the poem 'In the Small Hours'); but, as in 'Old Furniture', which also speaks of the pleasures of dancing fingers and the 'airy quivers' of a bow, the poet knows that he must move on:

> Well, well. It is best to be up and doing,
> The world has no use for one to-day
> Who eyes things thus – no aim pursuing!

Hardy even concedes the likelihood that he sins against the younger generation by trying to relive the past:

> I should not have shown in the flesh,
> I ought to have gone as a ghost; . . .
>
> But to show in the afternoon sun,
> With an aspect of hollow-eyed care,
> When none wishes to see me come there,
> Was a garish thing, better undone.
>
> ('He Revisits his First School')

He offers readers no single key to his response to the past. 'Concerning his Old Home' – sixteen lines – reproduces a different mood for each quatrain. He himself changes; he knows that others have seen him as different 'specimens of man' ('So Various'); why should the truth about what he recalls, or the mood which tinges the recollection, be any less complex, any less 'various' in their 'pith and plan', than his own incarnations over the years? (The question, rhetorically shaped, suggests its own answer.)

Taking the longer view, he knew that whatever happiness he experienced was fragile ('He Fears his Good Fortune'); would have to be fought for ('A Self-Glamourer'); and would ultimately collapse under the weight of years ('Life Laughs Onward'). He had learned 'what Earth's ingrained conditions are' ('Seventy-four and Twenty'). His interest in studying his family tree ('The Pedigree') led finally to the characteristic thought that countless generations of his 'sire-sown tree' had shaped his character; in important respects he was never a free agent. He had witnessed a change in standards of taste (in the poem 'An Ancient to Ancients' he notes that 'the bower we shrined to Tennyson . . . is roof-wrecked'). He sought satisfaction in 'years of moderate gladness / Mellowed by sundry days of sadness', and, 'little endowed', he tried not to want more than a 'private man' might reasonably ask for ('A Private Man on Public Men').

In such poems of reminiscence his tone is not idly yearning for a vanished Golden Age. He knows what he knows; he has acquired wisdom through a perilous journey, though he may never have had the power to direct his own destiny. Why, then, should he reshape the past? Falsify it by sentimentalising either its promise or what – to a poet in his seventh decade – it actually brought?

> O what's to me this tedious Maying,
>   What's to me this June?
> O why should viols be playing
> To catch and reel and rigadoon?
> Shall I sing, dance around around around,
>   When phantoms call the tune!

('Song to an Old Burden')

It is now too late for regrets, he told himself. The melody had ended, and the only dancers are 'phantoms'.

Hardy's reasons for being discreet are understandable, and have to do with the special circumstances of his life. But Hardy is not all that indirect or oblique. For Hardy, being honest to himself was enough. The more we know about Hardy's life the better fitted we are to read between the lines; yet, even without such knowledge, we close the *Collected Poems* with a sense that we have seen the poet plain. He reveals himself – perhaps despite himself – in the alternating sequences of 'grave, positive, stark delineations' and 'those of the passive, lighter, and traditional sort presumably nearer to stereotyped tastes'.[39]

4

The Occasional Poems

A discussion of Hardy's occasional poems, written during relatively relaxed moments for or about friends, special moments in history, and on request, is not necessarily trivial in its concerns. Hardy's work is rewardingly prismatic no matter what the subject; every topic is potentially related to a large number of allied interests, and some of those interests are central in any consideration of Hardy's way of thinking. Nevertheless, grandiose claims for the intrinsic value of these poems should not be made. In one sense every poem written by any poet may be described as 'occasional', as a response to a set of circumstances that, better known and more precisely defined, may render difficult the judgement that any other way of responding would have been equally valid. Let me, rather, define the term 'occasional' as describing a poem that denotes a minor effort or encapsulates a passing mood, and is clearly identifiable with a given year or event; a poem, in other words, that would not have been written much earlier or later.

Now, quite apart from the fact that such a definition would apply to all of Hardy's war poems (which are considered in Chapter 8), two comments seem in order: one, that Hardy saw nothing demeaning in the writing of such poems, poems that he frequently would not have written without some kind of formal invitation to do so (he functioned, in other words, as an uncrowned poet laureate living in Dorset); and two, that he enjoyed writing them. Their zest should not be underestimated; they come into existence as live and kicking poems; their tone, taken over all, is more cheerful and affirmative than many of the poems among which they nestle.

Let me begin with a poem written for an audience of 'disabled' soldiers and sailors, 'The Whitewashed Wall', that first appeared in *Reveille* (November 1918). The editor who had requested it was John Galsworthy. Although nothing about the military way of life is alluded to within the poem, its message – that love remembers and immortalises when all others forget – must have been all the more powerful because of the indirectness of Hardy's art. For the benefit of those who do not immediately recall the event of the poem, it is basically the story of a boy who, sitting by the fire, once cast his shadow on the chimney-corner wall; a friend drew his 'lifelike semblance' in pencil there; and accidentally, some time later,

> The whitener came to cleanse the nook,
> And covered the face from view.

But the mother always remembers 'he's there', and often turns towards the wall to kiss his remembered image,

> As if entranced to admire
> Its whitewashed bareness more than the sight
> Of a rose . . .

Whiteness may cover us over, hide us from life. The son, we are told, is buried 'under his sheet of white'; and although the painter sees no alternative ('When you have to whiten old cots and brighten, / What else can you do, I wonder?'), his role is that of gravedigger; only our memory keeps our loved and absent ones alive, preserves their human dignity. 'The Whitewashed Wall' is, in its simple language and its respect for the sacredness of 'this raptured rite' (the kiss which the mother repeats in her 'shy soft way' whenever she turns to the wall), a restatement of Hardy's view that immortality is achievable only through the remembrance, generation after generation, of one who deserves to be remembered. Such was the burden of 'Her Immortality' (*Wessex Poems*) in which the ghost of a 'dead Love', conjured up by the thoughts of the lover who is still alive, reminds her living sweetheart of his fearsome responsibility:

> 'A Shade but in its mindful ones
> Has immortality:
> By living, me you keep alive,
> By dying you slay me.'

The appalled lover in this relatively early poem thus learns that through himself 'alone lives she', and that when he dies, her spirit too will end 'its living lease, / Never again to be!'

The matching poem, 'His Immortality' (*Poems of the Past and the Present*), is dated February 1899 and suggests that the process of dying may well be a slow fading-away of memories; instead of the 'second death' of 'Her Immortality', i.e. a *sudden* obliteration of the beloved when the man who loved her passes from the earth, Hardy suggests in 'His Immortality' a protracted erosion from 'each faithful heart' later, from 'his fellow-yearsmen', who also grow old and die; and finally, even from the 'I' of the poem:

Lastly I ask – now old and chill –
If aught of him remain unperished still;
And find, in me alone, a feeble spark,
Dying amid the dark.

And such is the burden of 'The To-be-Forgotten', the poem which
Hardy placed directly after 'His Immortality', in which 'a small and sad
sound' from the tombs laments 'the second death' (Rev. 20:14); so long
as a soul on earth keeps a 'loved continuance / Of shape and voice and
glance', so long as memory continues, the dead are immune to 'oblivion's
swallowing sea'.

'The Whitewashed Wall' does not argue for the truth of a different
concept of time and memory. Hardy's bleak concluding statement of 'A
Sign-Seeker' (*Wessex Poems*), although attributed to 'Nescience', was
substantially his conviction through all the years that followed his
religious crisis of the late 1850s: 'When a man falls he lies.' Hardy held, in
brief, no faith in after-life as convinced Christians conceived it:

I have lain in dead men's beds, have walked
    The tombs of those with whom I had talked,
Called many a gone and goodly one to shape a sign,

    And panted for response. But none replies . . .

He never denied that others, 'rapt to heights of trancelike trust', were
entitled to 'read radiant hints of times to be', and to believe in personal
immortality (and Hardy may have well remembered Tennyson's impassioned hope against hope, in '*In Memoriam*', that he would some day be
reunited with Hallam: in Hardy's phrase, 'heart to heart returning after
dust to dust'). But Hardy found that 'such scope' was 'granted not to
lives like mine . . .' and there is no evidence that Hardy's persona in 'A
Sign-Seeker', a deeply troubled, religiously uncertain modern, was a
dramatic creation; everything he says is consonant with Hardy's personal
views. Like Shelley, Hardy would have willingly believed, could he have
seen 'those sights of which old prophets tell', but those sights were
denied him. As with Unamuno, a contemporary Spaniard, faith was
impossible if he could not believe in a resurrection after death of the
body, of the identity of the individual self.

Even so, the tone of 'The Whitewashed Wall' is gentler. The difference
has to do with Hardy's respect for the mother, observed by an acquaintance who has 'known her long', but has only recently seen 'this
raptured rite' of her kiss to an image long since painted over, which
contrasts appealingly with the heavily clanking and lugubrious self-

concern of the earlier poems. Others may not see the image, but *she* 'knows', and her knowledge is deeply held; rational argument cannot persuade her otherwise; and as Hardy once wrote (18 February 1920) to a Mr Joseph McCabe, who was proposing to include him in a *Biographical Dictionary of Modern Rationalists*, '. . . he thinks he could show that no man is a rationalist, and that human actions are not ruled by reason at all in the last resort.' The poem accepts the right of a mother to treasure memories that sustain her; the whitener has indeed 'covered the face from view', but the painter's imagination is limited, and his is not the last word. We conclude the poem knowing that the intended audience of this poem in *Reveille* must have felt reassured that what they had been – their shadows – would similarly be remembered by those who loved them. As an occasional poem, it worked because Hardy filled it with genuine feeling.

It is possible to say that almost any poem of Hardy's late period opens up possibilities of a review of an entire lifetime. Although full study of these occasional poems would require time and space disproportionate to my sense of their intrinsic artistic value, three categories of these poems should be identified, because in these – the first, in which literary debts are generously acknowledged; the second, in which Hardy meditates on the essence and accidents of Time; and the third, in which he reflects on the headline events of journalism – Hardy seems to be rendering some final, and surprisingly positive, judgements.

Hardy's reading tastes are closely related to the quality of the education that he shaped for himself in mid-century Dorchester; the broad out-lines of that educational process have been defined in Chapter 1. One example of his unflagging enthusiasm for learning may be cited here, as a reminder: his remark that nearly all his readings in the Greek *Iliad* 'had been done in the morning before breakfast'.[1] Those who respect Hardy's literary achievement do not need to dramatise it by denigrating the quality or the extent of his formal education. Whatever our criteria for evalu-ation, that education served Hardy well all his life. F. R. Southerington has phrased it well: 'Those who look closely at Hardy's education, taking full account of the available alternatives, may wonder more at its fullness than its deficiencies.'[2]

What has become apparent with the passing of more than three decades since the original publication of Carl Weber's biography, *Hardy of Wessex: His Life and Literary Career*,[3] is that the Appendices on 'Hardy's Debt to Browning' must be read in conjunction with a good many widely-scattered special studies of Hardy's relationships to earlier and contemporary writers. The subject of Hardy's literary affiliations is very large, and perhaps impossible to define once and for all. He was a diligent reader. He did not retain all the books that he bought. The Memorial Library, kept in the reconstructed study at the Dorset County Museum, Dorchester, is by no means complete. Many of the sets of authors' collected works in that Library were purchased late in Hardy's life (individual works had been read in different editions at earlier points of time); countless books were dispersed by sale, auction, and donation. The records of these events are incomplete, as they probably are for any man who collects books for a working library. Moreover, a large and irrecoverable fraction of Hardy's reading was in periodicals, in items picked up and discarded while travelling, and in the British Museum.[4]

Hardy paid homage to the past, and fairly acknowledged what he had borrowed or adapted for his own purposes in art. Of his late poems, three were given over to Shakespeare ('To Shakespeare after Three Hundred Years', in *Moments of Vision*), Byron ('A Refusal', in *Human Shows*), and Swinburne ('A Singer Asleep', in *Satires of Circumstance*). The tribute to Shakespeare is an Arnoldian kind of tribute: 'Bright baffling Soul, least capturable of themes.' Prepared as an offering for a tercentenary celebration in 1916, the poem moves slowly through a series of conventional statements: Shakespeare lived 'a life of commonplace', remained anonymous despite his art, and (from the perspective of a later age) had a 'strange mind'. The second, a comment on the Dean of Westminster's refusal to allow the placing of a memorial tablet to Lord Byron in the Poet's Corner of the Abbey (1924), is cast in the form of a dramatic monologue by the Dean himself. The third is a poem prompted not merely by a visit paid in March 1910 by Hardy to Bonchurch, on the Isle of Wright, where Algernon Charles Swinburne lay buried ('In this fair niche above the unslumbering sea'), but by several decades of reading and admiring Swinburne's verse, as well as a series of personal encounters and exchanges of letters that had developed a serious friendship between two distinguished men of letters.

If, on the basis of Thomas Hardy's tributes, one were to attempt to define the nature of the literary achievement of these three poets, he would have to settle for a series of singularly bland definitions. Shakespeare, for example, created an 'artistry' of 'penned dreams', his 'harmonies' have cowed 'Oblivion', and his creative imagination has 'lodged' as 'a radiant guest' in the larger world of 'man's poesy'. It would be even more difficult to understand – in the doggerel couplets of 'the grave Dean of Westminster' – why Byron should have been selected by anybody for immortalisation in Poet's Corner: so far as the Dean is concerned, Byron, Shelley, and Swinburne are all unfit for the Abbey, because they are 'rapscallions', 'sinners', creed-scorners. More of the reasons why Swinburne should be accounted a great and worthy poet are provided: Hardy speaks of his *Poems and Ballads* (1866) and other early works as 'new words, in classic guise', filled with passion:

> Fraught with hot sighs, sad laughters, kisses, tears;
> Fresh-fluted notes, yet from a minstrel who
> Blew them not naïvely, but as one who knew
> Full well why thus he blew.

But on closer examination these lines suggest merely that Swinburne wrote as a craftsman, and that his content was emotional; nor are we much illuminated by an extended account of a spiritual meeting between Swinburne and Sappho, 'his singing-mistress' whom Swinburne, as a 'disciple true and warm', acknowledges.

The subject-matter of these three occasional poems, indeed, is not the poets at all, certainly not as individuals with idiosyncratic styles or with a message for mankind. They are, rather, poets at odds with their environments, misunderstood by their contemporaries. Shakespeare is remembered by his fellow-townsmen in Stratford as 'a worthy man and well-to-do', somewhat remote (since he led 'elsewhere' the major part of his life), a neighbour willing to nod his good-day to others, but known primarily by reputation (though his achievements as actor-manager and playwright are never specified):

> 'Ah, one of the trademan's sons, I now recall. . . .
> Witty, I've heard. . . .
> We did not know him . . . Well, good-day. Death comes to all.'

As for Byron, his immortality had disqualified him from sharing in the 'distressingly small' space left in Poet's Corner (as Herbert E. Ryle, the Dean of Westminster, expressed it in his letter to *The Times* on 19 July 1924); for the Abbey was 'the best minster' in Great Britain; the Dean was concerned with any interference with his 'proper sphere'; and although some notorious figures already lay buried within Westminster, another like Byron would 'mean distortion'. From the Dean's indignation at this popular movement for making the grayness of the Abbey 'environ / The memory of Byron' it is impossible to gather any certainty that, in fact, the Dean is familiar with Byron's poetry.

For most readers the most poignant and interesting section of 'A Singer Asleep' may be stanzas II–V, in which Hardy reminisces about his thrilling discovery – his 'quick glad surprise' – during 'that far morning of a summer day' in the 1860s when he first encountered Swinburne's poetry. Swinburne's poetry came as a shock to 'Victoria's formal middle time', for 'his leaves of rhythm and rhyme', 'freaked with musical closes', had fallen, as from the sun, like 'a garland of red roses' about 'the hood of some smug nun'. The inevitable consequence was 'brabble' and 'roar' from unprepared readers, a 'fitful fire of tongues'. At the time of the composition of Hardy's tribute, more than four decades later, the power of those critics and hostile readers 'is spent like spindrift on this shore', while Swinburne's power 'swells yet more and more'.

As in 'The Whitewashed Wall', where a dramatised meditation on the meaning of immortality suggests (however faintly) Hardy's continuing concern with the ability of his own literary reputation to endure, these poems testify to the failure of the Philistines of Great Britain to appreciate the great writers who have come to live among them. The image of an exotic, foreign bird that mingles briefly with 'the barn-door brood awhile' before it vanishes 'from their homely domicile' (in 'To Shakespeare') is central to the meaning of all three outbursts. Hardy, here as elsewhere, was contemplating himself, as a novelist who had offended – most of the time without intending to or being conscious that he was doing so – over-sensitive and occasionally hypocritical readers; that he regarded these readers as not only directly responsible for his having renounced novel-writing after the uproar that greeted the publication of *Jude the Obscure*, but for the generally low standards of the craft of fiction (see, in particular, his essays on 'Candour in English Fiction', 1890, and 'The Science of Fiction', 1891); and that Hardy, in his final years, had not so much changed his attitude toward the general run of critics and reviewers as ceased to entertain the possibility of large-scale exceptions to the rule of their incompetence and malice. Although no single book by Hardy was reviewed in a majority of cases by hostile and obtuse commentators, he had a large number of such reviews and he believed that he had suffered enough; often his friends seemed to join the baying pack (Frederic Harrison's attack on his 'monotony of gloom' in the *Fortnightly Review* in 1920 proved particularly nettling, and Hardy wrote a bitter paragraph on both Harrison and Joseph Hone in the 'Apology' that he attached to *Late Lyrics and Earlier*, 1922); and Hardy was well aware of the mean-spirited attacks that were being made on him by George Moore and G. K. Chesterton.

As a young man, Hardy remembered the 'staggering' impact of a 'slating' that had appeared in the form of a *Spectator* review (1871) of *Desperate Remedies*. 'He remembered', the *Early Life* tells us, 'for long years after, how he had to read this review as he sat on a stile leading to the eweleaze he had to cross on his way home to Bockhampton. The bitterness of that moment was never forgotten; at the time he wished that he were dead.'[5] (He alluded again to the stile on 12 October 1922.)[6]

During Hardy's visit to Oxford in 1920 (mentioned in the preceding chapter) Charles Morgan, his guide (and at the time the manager of the Oxford University Dramatic Society), inquired why Hardy's stage-version of *Tess* had been put into a drawer, and why Hardy had no intention of allowing it to be performed. Hardy characterised dramatic criticism as superior to literary criticism: dramatic critics, he observed, had less time to rehearse their prejudices. He then went on to discuss literary criticism. Morgan duly noted that the bitter flavour of the discussion had originated in the past where, he believed, there 'was indeed good reason for it, but it was directed now against contemporary critics of his own work, and I could not understand what general reason he had to complain of them. He used no names; he spoke with studied reserve, sadly rather than querulously; but he was persuaded . . . that critics approached his work with an ignorant prejudice against his "pessimism" which they allowed to stand in the way of fair reading and fair judgment.'[7]

One of Hardy's final jottings (16 October 1926) in his second notebook placed both dramatic and literary critics on the same low level.[8] Hardy looked over the literary scene in both England and America and discovered no 'great critic' who could think for himself 'instead of following the lead'. As W. M. Parker recalled, Hardy believed that 'Saintsbury had read too much, and he did not possess sufficient insight.'[9] Hardy wrote to Sir Arthur Quiller-Couch on 22 December 1916 that there was 'no school or science of criticism – especially in respect of verse' (*The Thomas Hardy Year Book, No. 4,* p. 80). He certainly did not regard Arthur Bingham Walkley, who in the *Times Literary Supplement* (29 January and 12 February 1904) had reviewed *The Dynasts* as essentially a puppet-play, as a perceptive critic. Hardy, in responding to Walkley's interpretation, refused to match the friendly-humorous tone of the original review: 'Your critic is as absolute as the gravedigger in *Hamlet*', he wrote, and proceeded, in a second letter that was published in the *TLS* on 19 February 1904, to argue that 'the truth' seemed to be 'that the real offence of *The Dynasts* lies, not in its form as such, but in the philosophy which gave rise to the form'.[10] Since Walkley had not focused on the question of Hardy's 'philosophy', the response, however eloquent, was more than a little unfair, and symptomatic of Hardy's obsessive conviction that critics were blinded by the issue of his 'pessimism':

Worthy British Philistia, unlike that ancient Athens it professes to admire, not only does not ask for a new thing, but even shies at that which merely appears at first sight to be a new thing. As with a certain King, the reverse of Worthy, in the case of another play, some people ask, 'Have you read the argument? Is there no offence in't?'

This sense of identification with poets who, like himself, had been mis-understood, was to some extent self-dramatising. It did not render justice to those who did appreciate Shakespeare, Byron, and Swinburne during their lifetimes and beyond; moreover, it ignored the aesthetic and artistic grounds on which the work of these poets had been censured. But it was a fixed, significant element in the thinking of his final years, and should be characterised as sombre.

Two poems in *Winter Words* conclude the story: 'So Various', an amused series of character-sketches of himself as a changing and ageing poet, and 'Not Known', a poem written in 1914 'after reading criticism' but pub-lished for the first time in Hardy's final volume of poems. But the word 'amused' must be used carefully; Hardy, describing the ways in which his true self seems to change as the years pass, knows far better than his auditor, the 'you' of the poem, that 'all these specimens of man, So various in their pith and plan', have been from the beginning '*one* man', but the interpretations of his character which fragment his personality, which see him as somehow different from year to year, are only fitfully risible. Some of these interpretations have damaged his self-esteem; he knows that he has been considered 'a dunce', on other occasions possessor of 'a blank' of a brain, again as a man 'who never could have known true gladness', or as 'unadventurous' ('slack deeds / And sloth'), or as too dull to be worth satirising, or as the owner of a long memory ('one who for-got slights never'). Hardy's application of the moral to the kind of writer he saw himself to be – consistent, sincere, a man of integrity – is obvious enough; the outside world, the world of critics, saw him in different guises and missed the honest face beneath the mask. The poet's amuse-ment is genuine, but slightly sour.

The thought of the second poem is substantially the same: the 'phasm' that critics name as Hardy is as insubstantial, as unreal, as 'the wilings of the world' or 'the lastest flippancy', but Hardy refuses to acknowledge that he is what critics think him to be in any significant respect, not even in

> A single self-held quality
> Of body or mind.

And all visitors to the Dorset County Museum who have looked into the clipping-scrapbook entitled 'T. H. Personal' have seen, and wondered at, the carefully penned comments of disgust, anger, and flat contradiction in the margins of critical reviews, purported records of interviews, and assessments of his literary achievement based upon a reading – regarded by Hardy as faulty – of his 'true' self.

Occasional poems that deal with Hardy's strong sense of time inevitably overlap with poems of the final category, for in one sense all Hardy's poems are rooted deep in a tenaciously retentive memory of where he was at the given moment that the germ of an idea for a lyric or a meditation was born. There was the moment, for example, when Hardy visited the Albert Memorial Museum at Exeter and saw the skeleton of a fossilised bird ('In a Museum'); the fancy that the bird was musical, or 'cooed', was natural enough; but what science can or cannot confirm seems less significant than Hardy's speculation that whatever sound *Archaeopteryx macrura* made continues to reverberate somewhere, 'mid visionless wilds of space . . . / In the full-fugued song of the universe unending'.

A view of time as 'a dream', fabricated reality that dissolves as soon as we recognise the fraudulent lines of division between Then and Now, does not necessarily conflict with Hardy's more controversial, and certainly better known, view that any individual man or woman is insignificant because a given life-span is so limited in relation to geological time. We recall that frightening moment in *A Pair of Blue Eyes* when Knight, blown to the very edge of the Cliff-Without-A-Name, stares at a stony-eyed trilobite as he clings for his life to a weak support six hundred feet above the sea:

Time closed up like a fan before him. He saw himself at one extremity of the years, face to face with the beginning and all the intermediate centuries simultaneously. Fierce men, clothed in the hides of beasts and carrying, for defence and attack, huge clubs and pointed spears, rose from the rock, like the phantoms before the doomed Macbeth. They lived in hollows, wood, and mud huts – perhaps in caves of the neighbouring rocks. Behind them stood an earlier band. No man was there. Huge elephantine forms, the mastodon, the hippopotamus, the tapir, antelopes of monstrous size, the megatherium, and the myledon – all, for the moment, in juxtaposition. Further back, and overlapped by these, were perched huge-billed birds and swinish creatures as large as horses. Still more shadowy were the sinister crocodilian outlines – alligators and other uncouth shapes, culminating in the colossal lizard, the iguanadon. Folded behind were dragon forms and clouds of flying reptiles: still underneath were fishy beings of lower development;

and so on, till the lifetime scenes of the fossil confronting him
were a present and modern condition of things. . . .

Knight, the geologist whose eye has been trained to recognise the generations of created beings so that this reverie, at the moment of maximum
danger to himself, is wholly plausible, recognises the simultaneity of all
life-forms, and he understands, more keenly at that moment than ever
before (or afterward), that 'the dignity of man' is a chimera, that 'zoo-
phytes, mollusca, shellfish . . . the highest developments of those ancient
dates' are 'mean' relics, and that if he is to die, he will be 'with the small
in his death'.

Hardy pondered the meaning of time in a large number of poems, and
even as we concentrate on his last five volumes, a consistent pattern of
attitudes emerges. In *Satires of Circumstance*, the opening poem, 'In Front of
the Landscape', speaks of time as holding a series of 'infinite spectacles', as
a 'tide of visions' that overwhelms the poet; nothing that has passed is
lost; memories become 'lost revisiting manifestations'. In the haunting
'After a Journey', written to commemorate a visit to Pentargan Bay
(where Hardy and Emma Gifford had spent pleasant moments together
more than four decades earlier), the poet moves past 'Time's derision' to
become as he was before ('I am just the same as when / Our days were a
joy, and our paths through flowers'), to re-enter Emma's 'olden haunts
at last'. 'The Two Soldiers' who meet remember 'a memory-acted scene'
as vividly as if it had taken place a moment before rather than all 'those
years gone by. . . .'

'In a Museum' is not the only poem in *Moments of Vision* that treats the
permanency of time remembered. 'Heredity' proudly claims, for 'the
family face', an ability to live on, 'Projecting trait and trace / Through
time to times anon, / And leaping from place to place / Over oblivion.'
The inheritable traits which pass from generation to generation are

> The eternal thing in man,
> That heeds no call to die.

Hardy does not deny the withering, crippling effects of Time on health
and beauty (as in 'The Faded Face'), but the best way to accommodate
oneself to the ruin created by passing hours is to remember, as vividly as a
poet's imagination will allow, the emotion of the original moment, and –
knowing that something will 'go amiss' – to reconcile oneself:

> '. . . let the end foreseen
> Come duly! – I am serene.'
> – And it came.

> ('He Fears his Good Fortune')

Thus, though time may not be arrested in its passing ('The Clock of the Years' tells us that ageing is an 'ordained' process), it can be meditated on, understood, and adjusted to. And in *Late Lyrics and Earlier*, 'Going and Staying' personifies Time as a broom-wielding apparition:

> Then we looked closelier at Time,
> And saw his ghostly arms revolving
> To sweep off woeful things with prime,
> Things sinister with things sublime
>   Alike dissolving.

Happy images that the poet wishes would stay, 'seasons of blankness' that the poet wishes would go, are all swept into oblivion; the indifference of Time to what is discardable (or salvageable) is, when properly appreciated, sublime.

Nevertheless, oblivion exists only if *we* forget what has been swept off, and Hardy believed, as 'The Whitewashed Wall' made clear, that it is possible to remember, imprinted on our mind's eye, things which have passed from the world. Perhaps Hardy's fullest statement to this effect is contained in two poems, 'The Absolute Explains' and its coda, 'So, Time', both printed in *Human Shows*. It is probable that here, as elsewhere, Hardy is remembering Emma without naming her, but if the autobiographical elements of the poems are ignored, the main message, that Time is misunderstood by all (save 'the sound philosopher') as a destroyer when, in fact, it is the preserver of all events and beings 'in the Vast', becomes even more luminous: Love is not stripped of her adornings, songs have not faded, roads stretch 'forwardly as at rear', and the 'ever memorable / Glad days of pilgrimage' are 'unhurt by age'. There is no age

> . . . since in a sane purview
> All things are shaped to be
>   Eternally.

Thus, as Hardy says, 'Time is a mock', and we have learned, in this century, to believe in it less, as a consequence of the writings of men like Einstein. (Hardy even names 'the Fourth Dimension'. Puzzled by writings on relativity, he had purchased and attempted to comprehend the drift of C. Nordmann's *Einstein and the Universe*, as well as *Relativity: The Special and the General Theory: A Popular Exposition*, a book which remains in the Dorset County Museum to this day. He accepted the notion of the relativity of motion, but Einstein's broodings, he thought, could lead one to 'think queerly of time and space . . .') Time is not so much a verbal construct as a 'toothless' simultaneity of past, present, and future:

toothless, presumably, because it does not wear down the sharpness of details of reality: and the Absolute, perhaps kindly, refuses to show the future to the poet because the scenes of life yet to come are too harrowing to behold 'all worked and shaped'.

It is not implausible to imagine Hardy yearning for the assurance of the Absolute; growing in conviction, toward the end of his life, that un-happiness over what has receded into the past wastes the energy and the courage one needs to face the 'phasmal' present; and hoping to become 'the sound philosopher' who has assimilated all the teachings of the Absolute. These hopes, no less powerful because they are veiled, underlie the occasional poems that Hardy liked to write about the summing-up of time-units, as at the end of individual years: 'End of the Year 1912' (*Late Lyrics and Earlier*), 'A New Year's Eve in War Time' (*Moments of Vision*), and 'At the Entering of the New Year' (*Late Lyrics and Earlier*). Regrets are coloured by the poet's cognisance of the impossibility of turning back the advance of time. If he remembers with regret his first wife, because she could not be with him to 'expend' a tear on the death of the same year in which she herself died (1912), his stance is 'lonely' rather than angry. If he reproduces in verse the true anecdote of 'a horse at mad rate', ridden by an unknown rider (Hardy suggests that his identity may have been Death) past Max Gate while the clock strikes midnight, it is only to conclude, resignedly,

> That the Rider speeds on
> To pale Europe; and tiredly the pines intone.

If 'At the Entering of the New Year', written 'During the War' – but presumably after 'A New Year's Eve in War Time', because its conclusion is so much more sombre (Hardy's word was 'pessimistic', though he despised it as a 'word beloved of the paragraph gents') – breaks into two parts, '(Old Style)' and '(New Style)', the division serves only to contrast the 'delight' of a more innocent time with the sighings of a 'bereaved Humanity'. It would be best if the gate to the future were to remain closed; but the poet knows that 'calm comely Youth, untasked, untired' will enter anyhow. The future will come when it will come.

Hardy, who thought of himself as an Ancient, had to achieve serenity of mind and purpose in the face of personal shocks as his friends and loved ones died, for he outlived so many; and during his final decade 'the shadows lengthened'.[11] Among those whose passings are recorded in the *Life* were 'his warm-hearted neighbour', Mrs A. Brinsley Sheridan; Handley Moule, the Bishop of Durham; Evelyn Gifford, 'Dear Evelyn!'; and in the chapter 'Some Farewells', the deaths of Charles Moule, last of the 'seven brethren', Elizabeth Allhusen, 'a charming girl', Mrs Florence Henniker, 'after a friendship of 30 years!', Sir Hamo Thornycroft, the sculptor, and, of course, Sir Frederick Treves, the distinguished surgeon in attendance on three reigning monarchs, whose life in so many ways intersected that of his fellow Dorsetman. A survey of Hardy's increasingly stoical reflections on the inexorable movement of Time might well conclude with a consideration of the poem 'In the Evening' that Hardy wrote on the day of Sir Frederick's funeral at Dorchester Cemetery, only four years away from his own.

The problem considered is older than Greek philosophy: why are we summoned into life, painful and ultimately disappointing as it is? The dialogue, between the doctor and 'a spirit attending', begins with a comment that the chalky soil of the cemetery is where Treves began his 'being, and the being of men all'. The doctor, puzzled, inquires why he could not have rested for ever 'amid the dust and hoar', since he 'knew no trouble or discontent', but there is no answer to such a question. (Hardy pretended to no more knowledge of metaphysical problems than he actually possessed; his poems were ' "questionings" in the exploration of reality . . . the first steps towards the soul's betterment, and the body's also.')[12] Yet the spirit tells the doctor that his soul left at the beckoning of Aesculapius, Galen, and Hippocrates, even if 'perhaps' Time itself did not send a signal that he had a need to be called to life. The final words of the spirit move away from the question that Treves has posed: 'Enough. You have returned. And all is well.' These words, slightly modified and condensed from the version published in The Times on 5 January 1924, a version that earned the honour of being carved on the monument erected over Sir Frederick's grave, suggests the nature of the truth with which Hardy finally learned to live. For Sir Frederick the turmoil of life had ended; good and necessary work had been accomplished; he had served his king and nation, and now dust returned to dust. There is about the poem not the slightest hint of regret or melancholy, and here, as in a few other poems written close to the end of a series of troubled musings on the nature of mortality, Hardy seems to have achieved a perilous but genuinely satisfactory relationship with the Time that, Janus-faced, revealed itself to man as both Destroyer and Preserver.

Hardy was not a journalist, and protested, on different occasions, that he had difficulty in writing poems to order, yet he frequently offered to an editor, with diffidence and after first entering his demurrer, a poem that he thought 'might serve' the occasion. A typical example is the way in which he submitted the lovely poem 'The Maid of Deinton Mandeville' to John Middleton Murry, editor of the *Athenaeum*: 'I have found some verses which at first I thought would only suit publication in a *daily* paper dated April 30th. But I find by accident there will be an *Athenaeum* on April 30th next, and therefore I shall have pleasure in sending you . . .' etc. Two observations on this category of occasional poems seem in order, however, since Hardy – a devoted newspaper reader, well posted on current events, and always alert to the odd and out-of-the-way anecdotes that in some way illuminated history – wrote more of them than a casual reader might suspect. They do not *look* like topical poems, for one thing; Hardy had a habit of universalising his poems, lest they bear too narrow and special an application. For another, they are not factional statements; it would be impossible to claim that any given poem committed Hardy's view to a specific political party.

'A King's Soliloquy', ascribed to King Edward VII on the night of his funeral (20 May 1910), tells us more about Hardy than about its presumed speaker. For it was the poet who would have preferred the anonymity of a profession he liked – to be 'a small architect in a country town',[13] or a cathedral organist (better than 'anything in the world')[14] – more than the notoriety associated with literary success. He spoke, however, in the voice of a King who would

> prefer the average track
> Of average men.

Hardy's voice behind the King's voice complained of the 'something, that bound hard his hand, prevented him from holding true to 'first thoughts'; Edward lamented the 'That' – the Immanent Will – shaping and planning his acts and himself. It is odd, given the occasion, that Hardy does not imagine the King either regretting his mistakes, or triumphing in the memory of his victories. Rather, it amounts to a confession of futility -' . . . what kingship would /It cannot do' – flavoured by regret that the King's role, his powers, and his pleasures have been grossly distorted by public misunderstanding; the 'theoretic view / Of regal scope' and the sighing-after of 'kingly opportunities' were, Hardy believed, unrelated to the reality of cloying 'pulse-stirrings', 'days of drudgery, nights of stress', and the carkings that beset a throne, 'even one maintained in peacefulness'.

It is, to say the least, an unexpected view of Edward VII, and the companion poem which follows it in *Satires of Circumstance*, 'The Coronation', is hardly the kind of Coronation Ode that Clement Shorter had in mind when he requested one. Hardy probably wrote it as partial penance for his turning down an invitation to attend the crowning of George V (22 June 1911), and escaping to the Lake District in order to avoid the crowds of London. Without reviewing the doggerel – which is in each case cleverly adapted to the known predilections of the deceased monarchs – we may note that Hardy concludes with the incisive line,

'Clamour dogs kingship; afterwards not so!'

The life from which they all have been freed is a burden (regarded as such both by themselves and by the poet); their 'dusty rest' in the Abbey, they feel,has been earned. It is not a major effort as a poem; it offers no striking or novel insight; but its outstanding feature is Hardy's sardonic, unimpressed commentary on what was regarded by his countrymen as a solemn occasion and an opportunity to begin afresh. Hardy knew that the new King would be haunted by the noise of the crowd, frustrated by the 'Prime Cause or Invariable Antecedent of "It" ', and ultimately anxious to be 'in darkness laid below'. The topical poem, in brief, became a restatement of how unchanging history really is.

Although this analysis may be repeated an indefinite number of times, two more occasions will serve to conclude this discussion. In the first, Hardy glanced obliquely at a political event of some consequence, the movement for 'the reconstitution of Palestine as a National Home for the Jewish people',[15] which he sympathised with to the extent of signing a declaration; yet the poem 'According to the Mighty Working', mentioned by Hardy in the same paragraph, and reprinted in Late Lyrics and Earlier, does not mention a specific event, movement, or political problem; the two stanzas (called 'verses' by Hardy) are generalised to cover all the agitation that inevitably breaks out when formal hostilities end ('Peace, this hid riot, Change. . . .'); and indeed Hardy, in responding to another of John Middleton Murry's requests for a topical poem, did not identify for Murry the relationship between the verses and the movement to reconstitute Palestine. It seems more likely that Hardy had fully as much in mind the letters he had received during the spring of 1919, 'from Quiller-Couch, Crichton-Browne, and other friends on near and dear relatives they had lost in the war', and that when Hardy employed the word 'relevant', he may simply have meant relevant to the problems created by the possibility of armistice. The date appended to the poem – 1917 – meant that what Hardy had written during the period of intense killing on the Western Front now served a host of purposes, and had a richly ambiguous applicability. It was – shall we say – a timely poem on a timeless concern, and Hardy ended his observations with an allusion again to a Will that escapes definition and even man's knowledge:

This spinner's wheel onfleeing,
Outside perception's range.

Hardy's compassion for the displaced Jews was a living concern at the time of his sending the poem to the *Athenaeum*, but a reading of the poem which stresses a particular political problem is reductionist.

Finally, the poem 'On the Portrait of a Woman about to be Hanged' deals with Mrs Edith Thompson, whose murder of her husband had been a newspaper sensation of the early 1920s, complete with a secret lover, love-letters, the administering of poison over a seventeen-month period, and a fatal stabbing. Hardy did not claim that she was innocent; the evidence presented in court had been damning; yet he knew that not all readers had been convinced, and there had even been a demonstration with placards defending her and her 'friend'. But he had been struck by her photograph; she had been, in Joseph Conrad's phrase, 'one of us', and in Hardy's rewording, 'one of our race', and she wore a 'gown of grace'. The mild-mannered expression, the 'innocent face', hid an evil, a 'tare' that had been sown 'in a field so fair'. She had become a Clytaemnestra in spirit, and here, at the bar of justice, an object of 'derision'.

Hardy did not know why she had committed murder, why this singular 'riot of passion' had taken place. A worm had been sent 'to madden Its handiwork' presumably by the same Immanent Will – the 'Causer' – that had originally made her 'sound in the germ', but Hardy held no conviction that she herself would ever know the reason; he implies that, given the inscrutableness of the workings of the Will, at one moment in time an equal possibility had existed that she might never have gone wrong; that the murder might not have been committed. The poem presents a melancholy prospect: behind any man or woman's face, homicidal thoughts might be 'drumming, drumming', and we will never know in advance who has been cursed, and who blessed, by the Will to which we all are subject.

So the topical poems turn out, on closer examination, not to be topical in their conception or their final appeal, and there is something vaguely reassuring about the spectacle of the poet evading categories, defying efforts to relate his poems to established traditions, and confounding critics who were always more comfortable with the book Hardy had published a decade earlier than the one just off the press. But Hardy knew that 'the night cometh' – it was one of his favourite quotations – and was not only impatient with misinterpretations of his intentions or what (he thought) he had so plainly said, but disturbed that some of his projects became increasingly difficult to realise as he aged. In the 'General Preface to the Novels and Poems' that he prepared for the Wessex Edition of 1912, he referred to his hope to create, in poetry, 'a fairly comprehensive cycle of the whole', a series of 'contrasting' sides of things: 'I had wished that those [poems] in dramatic, ballad and narrative form should include most of the cardinal situations which occur in social and public life, and those in lyric form a round of emotional experiences of some completeness.' He sighed, and went on to quote Browning's 'The Last Ride Together':

The petty done, the undone vast![16]

Yet if a few generalisations are warranted on the basis of this review of poems seeking to transfix a moment of time, to redeem it from dissolution in the vaster Flux, one would surely be that Hardy entertained that rarest of poetical gifts, what he called the faculty 'for burying an emotion' for as long as forty years, 'and exhuming it at the end of that time as fresh as when interred';[17] in brief, that poems about the past were as intensely lived in the process of creation as any poem about a given event or personal relationship in the present. In the larger sense, all his poems are 'occasional'. Moreover, they stress memory not only as the means of assuring immortality, as in 'The Whitewashed Wall', by means of which soldiers were reassured that their loved ones had not forgotten them, but as evidence that all ages, spoken utterances, and human beings who had ever lived could be restored by means of a moment's reflection; that death itself, when properly assessed, was an illusion; and that one did not need to be a Christian to so believe. And always at the centre of his poems about others – the artists of an earlier age, the distinguished surgeon, the beautiful murderess – we find the poet himself, wondering, reflecting, and finally accepting the view of truth that he had worked out for himself.

5

On the World of Nature, and of Living Things

'The Aërolite' may serve to open this consideration of Hardy's views on Nature. The poem tells us that 'a germ of Consciousness' once came to the world, perhaps from some wandering heavenly body (an aërolite); that it took root; and that the consequences of its quickening have been to make humanity conscious 'of stains and stingings'. It is an old dilemma: if 'mortal moan' is 'begot of sentience', would it not be better to get rid of 'this disease / Called sense, here sown', or in some way to 'limit its registerings to good'? Since neither solution is feasible within the foreseeable future – the question, as put, is academic – the poet proceeds on his way: 'I left [the seers] pondering.'

'The Aërolite' treats a fundamental element in what sometimes is incorrectly called Hardy's 'philosophy'. Efforts to define man's proper relationship to Nature occupied his thinking for a major part of his life. Once – stimulated by a review – he wrote a letter to *The Academy and Literature* (17 May 1902) to deny the basic premise of Maeterlinck's *Apology for Nature*. He thought it ingenious – a 'comforting fantasy', but 'sophistry – to argue, as Maeterlinck did, that the human race failed to perceive the justice practised by Nature on the basis of 'a scheme of morality unknown to us': pain and injustice suffered by generations who have preceded our own cannot be 'atoned for' by the 'future generosity, however ample', of a Nature that exercises 'unlimited power'. Hardy found no comfort in the possibility that Nature was blind 'and not a judge of her actions', or 'an automaton, and unable to control them', for beyond Nature, possibly a stage further back, responsibility must be assigned, and mankind will always want to know whom to blame: '. . . to model our conduct on Nature's apparent conduct, as Nietzsche would have taught', he concluded, 'can only bring disaster to humanity.'[1]

The arbitrariness of Nature, the suffering which exists on both large and petty scales, may be perceived by those who think and feel; the possession of consciousness, in brief, brings excruciating problems to today's generation, though ultimately sympathy may develop among future generations. The recurring irony of Hardy's world is that 'man, though evolved with and through the rest of nature, has none the less a consciousness which isolates and distinguishes him.'[2] The hope that consciousness will develop is, at best, a hope; in the meantime, and at present, consciousness is a decidedly mixed blessing for mankind.

So much is clear, and indeed standard in Hardy criticism. Hardy's concept of the relationship between human pain and a Supreme Law that changes slowly, though inevitably, has been ably defined by several admirers of Hardy, particularly in analyses of the canon since the Second World War. What is less well understood, however, is that the last five volumes of verse take for granted a reader's acquaintance with the explicit philosophical position of *The Dynasts*, and with at least a few of the earlier didactic poems; they are less insistent on man's inability to organise his institutions, less annoyed by the ironic disparity between aspirations and realities in a universe ruled by Immanent Will; they offer a less grating variety of didacticism. It is as if Hardy realised – after the publication of *The Dynasts, Part Third* – that he had converted the last of his listeners who might, through a reading experience, understand the hopelessness of direct challenge to the World Order. He was certainly tired enough as he went over the proofs of what he called '*Dynasts* III': 'It is well that the business is over, for I have been living in Wellington's campaigns so much lately that, like George IV, I am almost positive that I took part in the battle of Waterloo, and have written of it from memory.'[3]

'The Aërolite' is atypical in the final volumes not merely because it dabbles with the concept of the possibility of life on other worlds (Hardy often said that he had enough to do describing the many lives working out their destinies in the small corner of England that he had named 'Wessex'), but because its moral, or application, had been rendered so overtly. If the books beginning with *Satires of Circumstance* are separated from the earlier volumes of poetry, including *The Dynasts*, the growing gentleness in Hardy's tone would become more conspicuous. In what follows in this chapter I will consider two groupings of poems that have always seemed to me to be more prominent than the bald statements of doctrine which indeed did often dominate earlier collections: poems that deal, first, with Hardy's delight in the seasons and elements, in the natural world itself; and second, the world of living things, and man's relationship to animals and birds.

Even if the natural world seems unfriendly – with a 'sour spring wind', buds that pinch 'themselves together in their quailing', and a sun that

'frowns whitely in eye-trying flaps / Through passing cloud-holes' –
and, taken altogether, is frequently 'not commendable to-day', the poet
hopes for change, improvement: ' "Better tomorrow!" she seems to say'
('An Unkindly May'). The glum attitude toward Nature taken by the
science-fiction conceit of 'The Aërolite' does not darken the close-up
observations made by Hardy the naturalist. Those observations exhibit
Hardy in his happier moods. They are not merely documentary evidence
– as he finally put it – that he used to notice such things. They are poems
filled with wonder that the world is so various.

Their mood is often a more important element than content. The
poet is delighted by the 'daisy-and-buttercup land' into which he strays,
with its 'jungle of grass', the hedges that 'peer over, and try to be seen',
and the mead that 'is possessed of the neats'; in the last line we hear
about a woman who 'waits for her Love', but her identity is unclear, and
less important than that of the poet, who hymns – such is the title of the
poem – 'Growth in May'.

'A Backward Spring', written in April 1917, offers another testimonial
to the irrepressible hope of a countryman. Perhaps the sentiment is
unexceptionable: after 'frost and rime', the blooming of snowdrop,
primrose, and myrtle, the return of spring. Perhaps, too, the sharpness of
detail informing us of the 'timidity in the grass' is more vivid and memorable than any promise of the delayed season:

> . . . The plots lie gray where gouged by spuds,
>   And whether next week will pass
> Free of sly sour winds is the fret of each bush
>   Of barberry waiting to bloom.

The poet, afield, knows that some day the sun will shine and the warm
wind will blow. And even when the world seems farthest removed from
summer happiness – as in 'At Middle-Field Gate in February' – he never
denies the possibility of return of one more spring.

Like many nature poets Hardy was drawn to the easy contrast between
the sere months of late fall and the full burgeoning of spring. 'At Day-
Close in November', in *Satires of Circumstance*, is the central unit of three
linked poems. It follows 'Before and After Summer', with its cheery
lines,

> Looking forward to the spring
> One puts up with anything,

and it precedes 'The Year's Awakening', which asks both the 'vespering
bird' and the crocus root how they can be so certain that spring is on its

way. In 'At Day-Close in November' the 'beech leaves . . . Float past like specks in the eye', and the poet remembers how he planted the trees that now 'obscure the sky'. Children will never know that these tall trees were planted by any human hand; to them the trees have always been here. But the poem is not tinged by haunting memories of the poet's youth (easily imagined as running to this effect: I was young when 'I set every tree in my June time', and now I am old, and the leaves whirling down to the ground remind me that I, like them, must die). November in a nature poem by Hardy, in other words, is not the expectable analogue with human decay. If anything, the poet's mood is quietly proud and aware of accomplishment that has cheered not only himself but 'the children who ramble through here'. And what does that accomplishment amount to? He has contributed to, he has multiplied, the possibility of life. That is what he remembers in November.

He did not plant the trees solely for that reason, as readers familiar with the history of Max Gate will recall; the 'two or three thousand small trees, mostly Austrian pines', that Hardy installed grew rapidly and thickly, and soon provided the desired privacy from peering eyes: 'the house was almost entirely screened from the road, and finally appeared, in summer, as if at the bottom of a dark green well of trees'.[4] Bertie Norman Stephens, the gardener, was instructed not to cut too much or prune too diligently: Hardy 'did not like the outside world and wanted to be hidden from it', Stephens grumbled, and added, 'He was happiest when the trees were thick and tall, casing him in with their greenery.'[5]

Spring and autumn are the seasons praised in 'Weathers', the poem that opens *Late Lyrics and Earlier* and appropriately sets the mood for much that follows; but, in point of fact, Hardy likes aspects of *all* the seasons; some of his most vivid and beautiful lyrics treat summer and winter as well. The only point worth remarking is that this catholicity of taste lasted into *Winter Words*, though not at the expense of recognising the ills attendant upon inclement weather. 'The Robin' tells us of the inability of a bird to find a meal in an earth frozen by winter frost; finally it must die, turning 'to a cold stiff / Feathery ball!' 'The Later Autumn' sketches a sombre scene: 'Toadsmeat is mangy, frosted, and sere', while the spinning leaves, formerly so proud as they looked down on last year's dead leaves ('corpses'), find themselves forced to descend to 'huddle' on the ground 'in the same plight', while 'a robin looks on'. The ten thousand sheep at Pummery Fair are 'consigned to doom' as 'torrents fall' on the sodden pens ('A Sheep Fair'). 'The Faithful Swallow', determined to remain behind when his fellows migrated, now laments the cost:

> Frost, hunger, snow;
> And now, ah me,
> Too late to go!

Hardy, as a matter of practice, insisted that his maids feed the birds daily, and was particularly concerned about the ability of birds to fend for themselves in the wintry weather that (in a vivid phrase repeated by Florence) froze his own brains. 'I myself often feel very well in dry cold weather', the second Mrs Hardy said to Vere H. Collins, in her husband's presence, 'but my husband says that it is very thoughtless to say 'What a lovely frosty day" when one remembers all the suffering and cruelty it means to birds and other creatures.'[6] He kept close watch on the comings and going of birds at Max Gate. As he wrote to Mrs Henniker, on 22 December 1916, 'Our blackbirds and thrushes have had a hard time on account of the frost and snow, but they are recovering now.'[7]

Yet the final note is *hopeful*, however wan. Hardy is not averse to using the word, as in 'Snow in the Suburbs', with its concluding lines.

> The steps are a blanched slope,
> Up which, with feeble hope,
> A black cat comes, wide-eyed and thin;
> And we take him in.

Hope, and wonderment itself, as reflected in the watching eyes of 'The Fallow Deer at the Lonely House'; and acknowledged first on a window-ledge, then from the branches of 'the crooked neighbouring codlin-tree', as sweetly-whistling birds rejoice 'at being alive' ('A Bird-Scene at a Rural Dwelling'); and the trilling of 'a blackbird on a budding sycamore/ One Easter Day, when sap was stirring twigs to the core' ('I Watched a Blackbird'). The 'Nature poems' are not inconsiderable in number, they are notably homogeneous in tone, and their freshness and positiveness ought to be remembered in any summary of Hardy's thoughts about nature. A poem like 'I Am the One' (published posthumously) identifies its writer as a lover of nature who neither offends nor alarms ringdoves, 'up-eared hares', and 'wet-eyed mourners' as they move on 'to a hollowed spot'. The last stanza gives us the voice of the watching stars.

> I hear above: 'We stars must lend
>   No fierce regard
>   To his gaze, so hard
>   Bent on us thus, –
> Must scathe him not. He is one with us
>   Beginning and end.'

His faith in the organicism of Nature – i.e. all sentient things, the plant as well as the animal kingdoms, are interrelated – underlies his approval of the gardening interests of both his wives, his dislike of holly trees being torn apart for decoration, his replanting of a wild strawberry (taken from Scott's tomb at Dryburgh) and subsequent keen disappointment when the gardener dug it up and threw it away: '*He is one with us /
Beginning and end.*' And there is the piquant observation (made by Emma?), recorded by Sir James George Frazer in *The Magic Art* (1911), that 'the reason why some of his trees in front of his house at Max Gate did not thrive was because he looked at them before breakfast on an empty stomach.'

Mrs J. Vera Mardon, a musician of considerable skill, accompanied Hardy while he played his violin, and also helped to prepare music for several Hardy plays produced by the Dorchester Debating and Dramatic Society. Her witness adds a detail I have seen recorded nowhere else:

> Hardy was most at ease when alone in the countryside. There,
> isolated from human contact, he could think uninterrupted,
> except for the natural movement of trees, birds and beasts. He once
> recalled to me that on occasions when he was deep in the country
> and needed to jot down an idea, but had no paper upon which to
> write, he would make use of a large leaf or chip of wood from the
> woodman's axe.[8]

Indeed, Hardy's interest in looking carefully at the natural world affected the way people interpreted his appearance. He seemed to more than one onlooker to be surprisingly different from what might be expected of a famous author, 'a Classic'. On the occasion of a visit to Oxford (February 1920), Charles Morgan described his eyes as those of 'some still young man who had been keeping watch at sea since the beginning of time.'[9] Godfrey Elton, who showed him around Oxford during his visit to Queen's College in June 1923, characterised him as 'an elderly country gentleman with a bird-like alertness and a rare and charming youthfulness – interested in everything he saw, and cultured, but surely not much occupied with books. . . .'[10] And in January 1926, offering an excuse for resigning his Governorship of the Dorchester Grammar School, 'knowing that he was by temperament unfitted to sit on committees that controlled or ordained the activities of others', he spoke of himself in a phrase consonant with the images of 'I Am the One' and 'Afterwards': 'He preferred to be "the man with the watching eye." '[11] On his last birthday (his eighty-seventh), a cold June day, he rested in the library, alone, before a wood fire. Mrs Granville-Barker, in a letter written a few months later, recorded what she saw when she peeped in at him through the garden window: 'He was not asleep but sitting, walled in with books, staring into the fire with that deep look of his. The cat had established itself on his knees and he was stroking it gently, but half-unconsciously.'[12]

Hardy's interest in animals – which I should like to consider as preliminary to some reflections on Hardy's sense of the interrelatedness of elements of the universe – focused frequently on his dog Wessex. Although the tombstone of this 'famous dog' identifies the age of Wessex as more than thirteen years, Hardy, in *The Later Years*, speaks of the dog as 'having been the companion of himself and his wife during twelve years of married life', and Wessex, indeed, was not Hardy's dog so much as Mrs Florence Hardy's dog. Mrs A. Stanley, the cook at Max Gate, commented once, in a moment of bitter recollection, 'Hardy had a strong dislike of children and certainly when I was there, dogs. I once heard him say to his wife: "Two things that you have brought into this house that I dislike are the dog Wessex and Mrs Stanley's child." '[13] This blow to the sentimental stereotype of Hardy as a dog-lover must not be accounted as due to the pique of only one observer (however intimate with the doings of the Hardy household); other visitors noted Hardy's distaste for sacrificing personal comforts for the sake of a dog, and the niece of Hermann Lea, Joyce Scudamore, noted how a dog that barked – and that, of course, needed to be taken for walks – inevitably proved 'distracting' to Hardy's jealously guarded right to quiet. Mrs Hardy considered the introduction of Wessex into the household as one of her two big mistakes (the other mistake being the purchase of a pianola that she discovered she was unable to play while her husband was at home).

Wessex was a large, formidable-looking, and companionable dog, of the 'King Edward terrier' type. Ultimately Hardy not only reconciled himself to his presence but grew fond of him, walked him around the garden, took him for automobile drives, and boasted to visitors that Wessex, through some telepathic gift, could sense the moment of time when Mrs Hardy, finished with her visit to London, entered the return train at Paddington. One one occasion Hardy told Sir Newman Flower that 'Wessie' – as he was sometimes called – had predicted the death of a visitor, William Watkins. In general, visitors were wary of a dog that growled threateningly at them, disputed their right to mouthfuls of food, took over the drawing-room, and occasionally bit. (The postman, bitten three times, retaliated on one occasion by kicking out two of his teeth, which Mrs Hardy thought was 'distinctly cruel'.) Lady Cynthia Asquith summed up, with some asperity, her judgement that Wessex was 'the most despotic dog guests had ever suffered under'. It is a matter of speculation, therefore, why Hardy should have found this animal – never housebroken, as Mrs Hardy's earlier three dogs had been – worthy of a close and personal attachment.

The two poems on Wessex that Hardy wrote – 'A Popular Personage at Home', published in 1924, and 'Dead "Wessex" the Dog to the Household', published in 1928 – are both written from the point of view of Wessex himself. In the first, a poem which recognises the dog's dominance over his supposed master and mistress ('To take a walk of a mile or so / With the folk I let live here with me'), Hardy imagines how the 'dubious ray' that 'at times informs his steadfast eye' may be a philosophical reflection: this long-familiar scene may change, or even, Wessex imagines, that he himself might 'pass' as well as his master. In the second poem, Wessex, sleeping in an animal graveyard on the west side of Max Gate, 'outside the house', denies that he will reappear ever again:

> . . . Should you call as when I knew you,
> I shall not turn to view you,
> I shall not listen to you,
>   Shall not come.

The dog that shared his master's home had shared literally thousands of hours of time with him. As Hardy noted laconically in his autobiography, 'There were those among Hardy's friends who thought that his life was definitely saddened by the loss of Wessex. . . .' Yet the headstone characterised Wessex as 'Faithful. Unflinching', and Hardy, more than he wanted to admit publicly, confided to Sir Sydney Cockerell only two days after the dog's death that he hoped no one would ask him about Wessex, or mention his name.

Some years earlier Hardy hoped that Wessex would not catch the hare responsible for a good deal of damage to the vegetables and growing plants of his garden. He told his gardener, Bertie Norman Stephens, to let the animals carry on. Stephens grumbled: 'He was very fond of animals and birds, and would never allow me to trap or shoot them, however destructive they were to the fruit or vegetables. He insisted that I allow all birds to do as they liked in the garden. This attitude did not always please me, especially when some carefully cultivated fruit was destroyed.'[14]

On three separate occasions Hardy angrily delivered himself of opinions on those who could not understand the rights of animals and birds to their share of life's pleasures (limited at best). In *Humanity*, the Journal of the Humanitarian League (August 1910), Hardy contributed a note that might be read at a meeting celebrating the downfall of the Royal Buckhounds, an organisation dedicated to 'blood sports'. He admitted that his views on sport in general were 'what are called extreme':

> . . . that is, I hold it to be, in any case, immoral and unmanly to cultivate a pleasure in compassing the death of our weaker and simpler fellow-creatures by cunning, instead of learning to regard their destruction, if a necessity, as an odious task, akin to that, say, of the common hangman. In this view the hunting of tame stags is but a detail.

On reading an article in *The Times* (17 December 1913) entitled 'Performing Animals: The Psychology of Pain in Man and Beast', Hardy immediately wrote a lengthy letter of angry rejoinder, denying the contention of the 'Correspondent' that animals did not feel pain in the same sense as human beings. 'Quite possibly some animals may be, and are, trained for performances without discomfort to themselves', he began,

> but there is ample evidence to show that many trainers prefer short cuts to attain their ends, and that these short cuts are by the way of cruelty. I have been present at dog performances at country fairs, where the wretched animals so trembled with terror when they failed to execute the feat required of them that they could hardly stand, and remained with eyes of misery fixed upon their master, paralysed at the knowledge of what was in store for them behind the scenes, whence their shrieks could afterwards be heard through the canvas.

Hardy protested against the use of drugs on animals; denounced the caging of birds ('. . . the assertion that a caged skylark experiences none of the misery of a caged man makes demands upon our credulity'); and concluded with a strong peroration:

> It seems marvellous that the 20th century, with all its rhetoric on morality, should tolerate such useless inflictions as making animals do what is unnatural to them or drag out an unnatural life in a wired cell. I would also include the keeping of tame rabbits in hutches among the prohibited cruelties in this kind.[15]

And again, when the League for the Prohibition of Cruel Sports met at Taunton to protest against hunting and coursing as blood sports, Hardy lent his support to their advocacy of the drag and the mechanical hare as substitutes for live animals. His two-sentence endorsement was printed in *The Times* on 5 March 1927: 'The human race being still practically barbarian it does not seem likely that men's delight in cruel sports can be lessened except by slow degrees. To attempt even this is, however, a worthy object which I commend.'

Why – in a universe operated, to the best of Hardy's knowledge and in the fullness of his belief, by Darwinian principles of survival and natural selection – should he have responded so emotionally, and in admittedly so extreme a fashion, to the activities and statements of those who, seeking pleasure for themselves, treated the brute beasts of the field and birds of the air as inferior orders of existence? The answer, to be found in several widely-scattered statements, has to do partly with what Hardy perceived to be a failure of imagination on the part of human oppressors. The eyes of horses haunted him after he had walked through the streets: 'When afterwards I heard their tramp as I lay in bed', he wrote in a diary-entry for 13 July 1887, 'the ghosts of their eyes came in to me, saying, "Where is your justice, O man and ruler?" ' He became convinced, even before the writing of The Dynasts, that horses should not be employed in battle 'except for transport'; his reason – that 'Soldiers, at worst, know what they are doing, but these animals are denied even the poor possibilities of glory and reward as a compensation for their suffering' – was considered by many to be an example of 'unpractical tender-heartedness'.[16] He even speculated, in Swiftian temper, on the desirability of substituting 'the smaller children, say, of overcrowded families' for blood-sports: 'Darwin has revealed that there would be no difference in principle; moreover, these children would often escape lives intrinsically less happy than those of wild birds and other animals.'[17] The science of his age had made available to the barbarians new, ingenious, and 'treacherous contrivances'. Vivisection, now that the law of evolution had 'revealed that all organic creatures are of one family', no longer could manipulate 'any logical argument in its favour'.[18] So intensely did he detest the 'needless suffering' of animals about to be butchered that he left money to two societies – the Royal Society for the Prevention of Cruelty to Animals and the Council of Justice to Animals – 'to be applied so far as practicable to the investigation of the means by which Animals are conveyed from their Homes to the Slaughter-houses with a view to the lessening of their sufferings in such transit and to condemnatory action against the caging of wild birds and the captivity of rabbits and other animals.'

If a correct reading of Darwin's 'discovery' had, indeed, 'shifted the centre of altruism from humanity to the whole conscious world collectively', taking care of animals is the same as protecting our own interests, men and animals are no longer to be considered 'essentially different', and we would do well to remember that every living creature's death diminishes us. Two poems printed in *Moments of Vision* underscore the position. On one memorable occasion, Hardy tell us in 'A Thought in Two Moods', he was unable to distinguish between the white and green daisies of the field and the pink-and-white dress of his wife (here called 'Ethleen'); the colours blended together, 'combined / As varied miens of one',

> that, in some mouldering year,
> As one they both would lie.

In the other poem, 'The Wind Blew Words', written during the Great War, Hardy goes even further. He not only comes to learn how he has broken the law 'to kill, break, or suppress', and how he has become 'pathetic' and distressed as a consequence of his failure to honour the sacredness of created life – whether animal or human, whether near or far, whether white or a member of another race ('black, dwarfed, and browned') – but he apprehends a truth beyond any kind of empirical demonstrability:

> The wind blew words along the skies,
>   And these it blew to me
> Through the wide dusk: 'Lift up your eyes,
>   Behold this troubled tree,
> Complaining as it sways and plies;
>   It is a limb of thee.'

A tree, then, is an organic creature, and has life; as Hardy knew from his readings in Schopenhauer and Von Hartmann, the tree expresses will of its own, even if a lower order of will; it wills itself to be a tree; and what Hardy, as he aged, believed with deeper conviction was that it, no less than all varieties and other hierarchies of life, had rights to be, and to continue to live and develop. Hence his outrage, in a poem such as 'The Blinded Bird', that men should blind a bird with a red-hot needle to hear it sing. Their ignorance of where nerve-centres are localised does not excuse their barbarity. Can they not feel what the bird feels? Can they not imagine what it is to suffer?

  In these poems of indignation at the failure of men and women to recognise the oneness of the created universe there exists a recognition that poetry, by itself – whether it incarnates a mood, or is 'in a large degree dramatic or personative in conception' (as Hardy wrote in the preface to *Wessex Poems*), or even fulfils Matthew Arnold's ideal, i.e. it applies ideas to life – cannot change the nature and actions of human beings who are predisposed to act cruelly or thoughtlessly. 'The Blinded

Bird', in its essence an illustration of the meaning of I Cor. 13:4–7 and of St Paul's definition of the Christian virtues, speaks of wrong, indignity, 'grievous pain', and the 'eternal dark' that the mutilated bird will move through for the rest of its life; but Hardy's emphasis falls on the sublimity of the victim rather than the mindless sadism of the oppressor:

> Who hopeth, endureth all things?
> Who thinketh no evil, but sings?
> Who is divine? This bird.

In 'Compassion', a celebratory statement about the hundredth year of the Royal Society for the Prevention of Cruelty to Animals, Hardy – who knew well that the tasks of the Society were endless, that the final battle would not be won so long as 'helplessness breeds tyranny / In power above assail' – preferred to rejoice in the victories that had been won over a century's time 'in battlings, patient, slow', and to hope that more had been won, 'maybe', than we know. 'Compassion' is a melancholy vignette about a bird-catcher's boy who detests his father's trade as 'wrong' and destructive. The poet, though secure in his knowledge that the boy is right in both observation and judgement, provides the father with the argument – irrefutable at one level – that 'Birds must be caught'. The father's lot 'is such employ' fully as much as the child's lot is to learn his lessons. Moreover, when Freddy runs off to become a sailor, we learn that the parents are 'heart-sick', that 'all cheer' has 'dried' within them, that each hour is 'an ache'. When the false news comes that the bird-catcher's boy has returned on a 'wintry Christmastide', Hardy emphasises the excitement of the parents, the fact that their faces are 'aglow'. But Freddy, as we learn, has died that night at sea, and nothing has changed, nothing will change, in the way of life of his father. What Hardy thought of the caging of birds is clear enough from images in Tess and Jude, as well as from the comments to friends quoted in several memoirs and in the public statements already cited; but in the poetry of the final years anger as such was being tamped down, controlled, as if in belated recognition of the infinite slowness with which the genuinely Christian virtues were encouraged to develop by human beings who had their minds on other things.

This generalisation holds true even in relation to the strongly-worded but relatively crude poem 'The Lady in the Furs', one of Hardy's last efforts. This poem is an angry attack on the kind of woman who benefits from her husband's indulgence (her robe 'cost three figures'), the slaughter of 'feeble and afraid' animals by 'a cunning engine's aid', and underpaid factory labour ('midnight workers' whom she does not know personally). Hardy is overemphatic in his conclusion: the lady repeats a characterisation of herself, by others, that she is 'but a broom-stick, / Like a scarecrow's wooden spine', and makes plain the poet's conviction that she is coarsely bred. Speculation over the identity of the 'lady' should not distract us from a recognition that the 'lofty lovely woman' who willingly benefits from animal murder is as incapable of perceiving the need for enlarging her moral imperatives as the bird-catcher, the bird-blinder, or those of

> . . . throbless hearts, near, far, that hear no calls
> Of honour towards their too-dependent frail . . .

('Compassion')

We remember that Hardy, as a private man, did not relish open combat with the thousand varieties of boor and philistine who considered a man of letters as somehow public property, *their* public property. An analysis of the reasons why he preferred to avoid uninvited visitors to Max Gate would not be wholly irrelevant to a consideration of the question why the main artistic medium of his final years – these volumes of relatively short poems, more lyrical and personal than has long been recognised – treated so gently the molesters of animals, birds, and even plants whom he so detested in his heart's core; suffice for the moment to say that these poems are for the most part oddly gentle, even a little remote, from their announced subject-matter. It may be, as 'The Wind Blew Words' suggests, that awareness of the full blundering destructiveness of even well-intentioned human beings ('The pathetic Me I saw / In all his huge distress') has rendered the poet helpless before 'a surging awe / Of inarticulateness'. More likely, the persona of 'Afterwards', the poem Hardy used as conclusion for *Moments of Vision*, came as close to speaking for Hardy directly as any persona ever did, and the 'I' of that poem is, in several suggestive ways, an observer rather than an actor in the dramas of life. Understandably so, since Hardy, a 'tremulous' seventy-seven, feared that his own long life was moving towards its close. This is how Hardy wanted to be remembered by his neighbours, as 'a man who used to notice such things', not as an author, as one who had travelled beyond Casterbridge and Wessex. He did not even declare a sense of pride in being a neighbour, or a man of Dorset related to other men of Dorset; these matters were not what he believed he would be remembered for; and only on the horizon, for the reader aware of the date of composition of 'Afterwards' – 1917 – flickers the light of a wider world with its convulsive, anguished concerns. Ageing and tired, he allowed himself to indulge in the memories of turning seasons, and the structure of the poem – as it alludes to the different quarters and moods of the country-side – is brilliantly articulated. 'Afterwards' is, indeed, one of Hardy's ripest achievements. But the tone is also quietly melancholic, and the poet does not speak of himself as one who has achieved or suffered greatly. Rather, he recalls that he noted as 'a familiar sight' the swooping-down of the 'dewfall-hawk' 'upon the wind-warped upland thorn'. He saw hedgehogs in the dark, and like the 'innocent creatures' who have watched the 'full-starred heavens', 'he was one', Hardy writes elegiacally, 'who had an eye for such mysteries'. Nor did Hardy deceive himself that his efforts to protect the birds and the beasts had been of much avail; striving over the years that they 'should come to no harm', he knew all the time that 'he could do little for them; and now he is gone.'

The poetic value of 'Afterwards' lies – perhaps primarily – in the subtle variations of its iterative structure. Even so, Hardy marked it as one of two poems under the sombre heading 'Finale'. It accompanies (and follows) a poem reviewing the history of Hardy's relationship to Emma, his first wife, that bears the equally portentous title 'The Coming of the End'. 'Afterwards' is a characteristic late formulation, a recognition (if one chooses to regard it as such) of the relatedness of all created things to one another ('mysteries'). The poet admits that he cannot change brutish relationships and attitudes, though in the past, on several occasions, he tried, 'he strove'. He is, in a word, resigned to the fact that the known condition of the world prevails over personal standards of decency and sympathy.

And what else should an old man do? Unrealistic though it may be to expect that Hardy's final years would see him go raging into the night, yet one might have expected more, on the basis of the passion and the sincerity of Hardy's personal opinions on the cruelty of blood sports, the genuine emotion stirring beneath recurrent bird images of the novels, the compassionate lines about 'horses, maimed in myriads' at Borodino (*The Dynasts*, III.I.v), or the even more striking musing of the Chorus of the Years the night before Waterloo (II.VI.viii), when the poet, as God's spy, imagines what the coneys, the swallows, the mole, the lark, the hedgehog, the snail, and the butterflies must feel in the midst of war that destroys their homes and crushes out their lives:

> Trodden and bruised to a miry tomb
> Are ears that have greened but will never be gold
> And flowers in the bud that will never bloom . . .

'Afterwards', in short, was meant to serve as final signature. Hardy's tone, deliberately chosen at the end of his life – toward the dilemmas of birds and beasts in a man-controlled world that, in turn, is driven by the Immanent Will – is as diminished, as distant, as the 'bell of quittance' that he hears sounding 'in the gloom' (in the final stanza) when 'a crossing breeze cuts a pause in its outrollings. . . .'

6

The Queen of Cornwall

The last major creative work of Hardy's career was a play, *The Famous Tragedy of the Queen of Cornwall*. It holds a special interest not only because it illustrates a number of highly developed attitudes toward what a play should be like, but because it represents the final expression of an enthusiasm for theatre that Hardy had sustained for more than half a century. Begun in 1916 – after a visit to Tintagel with Florence, his second wife – the play derived its initial inspiration from a bemused reflection that similarities existed between the heroine and his beloved Emma, memories of whom came flooding back as he tramped around the castle ruins. As he wrote to Sydney Cockerell on 20 September 1916, 'I visited the place 44 years ago with an Iseult of my own, and of course she was mixed in the vision of the other.'[1] At the time he wrote, Hardy was apologising to Cockerell for his inability to continue work on the play. Poetic inspiration did not return until the spring of 1923, when he picked up the manuscript again. He wrote swiftly, and completed a revised version of the 770 lines – 544 of blank verse, 226 rhymed – in August; publication followed in November. For any writer *The Queen of Cornwall* would have been a notable achievement as verse-drama (Hardy knew it would never have a large audience) in this form; but for a poet of eighty-three, it was even more remarkable.

This 'New Version of an Old Story', as Hardy identified it on his title page, required neither theatre nor scenery. The stage, Hardy wrote, 'is any large room', and he went on, a little severely,

> round or at the end of which the audience sits. It is assumed to be the interior of the Great Hall of Tintagel Castle: that the floor is strewn with rushes: that there is an arch in the back-centre (a doorway or other opening may counterfeit this) through which the Atlantic is visible across an outer ward and over the ramparts of the stronghold: that a door is on the left, and one on the right (curtains, screens or chairs may denote these): that a settle spread with skins is among the moveables: that above at the back is a

gallery (which may be represented by any elevated pieces of
furniture on which two actors can stand, in a corner of the room
screened off).

Relying on the willing co-operation of the audience to assume the
existence of what the director and playwright had eliminated from the
very beginning, namely, the 'imitative scenery' of London productions,
Hardy went on to insist that 'the costumes of the players are the conventional ones of bright linen fabrics, trimmed with ribbon, as in the old
mumming shows.' The question naturally arises as to whether Hardy had
arranged the play for mummers, and denuded the stage of its easily
obtainable accessories, on the basis of a theory applicable to drama in
general, or on the basis of a conviction that such restrictions were useful
primarily for this particular kind of play. Evidence suggests that the
theory was meant to be generalised; by the mid-1880s, Hardy had become
sufficiently irritated by the conditions prevailing to hamper the efforts of
playwrights that he held little or no hope for the emergence of a serious
drama on the English stage. A review of the grounds of Hardy's irritation
is essential if we are to appreciate his sense of the aggressive originality of
The Queen of Cornwall.

One problem – the unscrupulousness of theatrical producers and
managers – affected Hardy as early as 1881, after he had written a dramatisation of *Far from the Madding Crowd*, a 'promising' idea for the stage: 'a
woman ruling a farm and marrying a soldier secretly, while unselfishly
beloved through evil and through good report by her shepherd or
bailiff.' Hardy sought the assistance of Comyns Carr, an art critic with
considerable knowledge of the London stage. He accepted Carr's sugges-
tions, and made some of his own, for example, that 'the rank of the
personages should be raised, particularly that Sergeant Troy should
appear as a lieutenant, and that in this case the name should be changed.'
An original character of a gipsy was written into the script. Understandably, then, Hardy was delighted to hear of the play's acceptance by the
manager of the St James's Theatre; of an impending production. What
happened next? Notification of rejection, and then, as Hardy explained in
a bitter letter to *The Times* (2 January 1882), 'Silence ensued until *The
Squire* is proclaimed by many observers as in substance mine. My drama is
now rendered useless, for it is obviously not worth while for a manager
to risk producing a piece if the whole gist of it is already to be seen by the
public at another theatre.' He was referring to Arthur Wing Pinero's new
play, *The Squire*, that had been rushed into production at the St James's
Theatre on 28 December 1881, and he repeated his charge of shady ethics

in a letter to the *Daily News* that appeared on the same day; it concluded with a ringing denunciation.

> Had my dramatisation of the novel never been in the hands of the St. James's company; had they by their own choice read the novel and transformed it into such a play as is now produced, I should have said nothing; but having had their attention drawn to the theme by my play; having practically adapted it; having been able to learn from it how sundry difficulties of the novel were to be got over for the stage, I venture to say that the whole transaction of producing *The Squire*, without my knowledge and after studying my play, and to do all this without a single allusion to my work in the playbill, is quite unjustifiable, and would be a discredit to the management of any theatre.

Carl J. Weber, Hardy's biographer, reviews this unpleasant quarrel with a gallant willingness to believe Pinero's denial that he had plagiarised Hardy's dramatisation, and suggests that Pinero may have been inspired to write a play on a similar subject after having talked to Kendal, one of the managers of the St James's theatre, who at some earlier point in time had discussed Hardy's play with his partner Hare. (Comyns Carr had submitted Hardy's manuscript to Hare.[2]) But the coincidences, including the gipsy in Pinero's version, were striking, and if Hardy did not institute litigation, the possibility that he detested vulgar court combat is at least as strong as Weber's suggestion that he felt his case was weak. Weber's hypothesis, at any rate, does not (and cannot) presume to measure the extent of Pinero's knowledge of Hardy's manuscript which, after all, was in the hands of someone Pinero knew personally.

The dismaying lesson learned by Hardy was that, despite late 1882 productions in both Liverpool and London of *Far from the Madding Crowd*, his dramatisation represented an expenditure of energy that might have been more profitably diverted to prose fiction. He was doubly galled because the lessons of dramatic technique had been hard-learned, and ultimately had required the services of a consultant. When the editor of *The Weekly Comedy* solicited his views on how modern theatre might be improved, Hardy wrote a crisp reply from the Savile Club (printed in the issue of 30 November 1889), that clearly indicated a smouldering resentment:

> As I have no practical acquaintance with the management of theatres, I fear that my opinion on how an English 'free stage' is to be attempted will have very little value. . . . At the contemporary theatre we see life as it cannot be, though sometimes, perhaps, as it

might advantageously be. . . . Nowadays, persons who were devoted
to the drama in their youth find as they approach middle age that
they cannot by any possibility feel deeply interested in the
regulation stage-presentation of life, their impression usually
being: First act – it may be so; second act – it surely is not so; third
– it cannot be so; fourth – ridiculous to make it so; fifth – it will do
for the children.

But beyond his immediate grudge extended a conviction that modern
plays, as staged, appealed to eyesight rather than the imagination, and his
prescription for a British *théâtre libre* set down, for the first time, the way
in which 'a new interest, depending on startling convictions of fidelity to
life', might be effectively presented:

Could not something be done to weed away the intolerable masses
of scenery and costume? A good many hundred people would
travel a good many miles to see a play performed in the following
manner: – The ordinary pit boarded over to make a stage, so that
the theatre would approach in arrangement the form of an old
Roman amphitheatre; the actors performing in front of it, and
disappearing behind it when they go off the stage; a horizontal
canvas for sky or ceiling; a few moveable articles of furniture, or
trees in boxes, as the case may be indoors or out; the present stage
being the green room. The costumes to be suggestive of the time and
situation, and not exclusively suggestive of what they cost.

This concept – of an audience surrounding the actors, not simply sitting
at one end of an elongated chamber watching events take place on a
proscenium stage – was intended to facilitate seeing the play. That
Hardy did not regard the concept as radical is evident from his insistence
that the play (he underscored the word) would then be seen 'as it was
seen in old times', and as it could not be seen now because of its 'accessories'.

Moreover, Hardy's willingness to endure a limitation of audience for
the sake of insuring the genuineness of that audience's interest in what
it paid to see – fit audience though few – was entirely consistent with his
proposal, made in a contribution to a symposium in the *New Review*
(January 1890), that 'Candour in English Fiction' might be aided by new
avenues of printing and distribution: 'a system of publication under
which books could be bought and not borrowed' (an inevitable reduction
of the sales then being made to Smith's and Mudie's); the printing of
'emancipated serial novels(s)' as 'a *feuilleton* in newspapers read mainly by

adults . . . as in France'; and magazines for adults, 'exclusively for adults, if necessary', and perhaps at least 'one magazine for the middle-aged and old'.

He tried twice more before the century ended, however: a mildly successful one-act adaptation of 'The Three Wayfarers' (1893) and a disastrous repetition of his experience with Pinero, this time a version of *Tess* (1895) that did not secure the necessary financial backing early enough; two rival versions were completed and staged in England and America (1897), and Hardy's dramatisation of *Tess* remained unproduced until 1924. When the *Pall Mall Gazette* asked him to contribute to a symposium (printed in the issue of 31 August 1892) an answer to the question whether he had 'at any time had, or now [had], any desire to exercise' his gifts 'in the production of plays as well as of novels', he answered, somewhat dryly, 'Have occasionally had a desire to produce a play, and have, in fact, written the skeletons of several. Have no such desire in any special sense just now.' Another question – 'Why you consider the novel the better or more convenient means for bringing your ideas before the public whom you address?' – stimulated a fuller reply, one that ticked off the reasons why playwriting seemed like an arid exercise to him, despite his appreciation of both Greek and Elizabethan dramatic literature. Plays in the late years of Queen Victoria's reign had to fit parts to actors, 'not actors to parts'. Managers would not risk 'a truly original play'. Scenes had to be arranged 'to suit the exigencies of scene-building'. (Hardy insisted that 'spectators are absolutely indifferent to order and succession provided they can have set before them a developing thread of interest.') All these constraints inhibited 'the presentation of human passions,' and stimulated excesses in production:

> the presentation of mountains, cities, clothes, furniture, plate,
> jewels, and other real and sham-real appurtenances, to the neglect
> of the principle that the material stage should be a conventional or
> figurative arena, in which accessories are kept down to the plane
> of mere suggestions of place and time, so as not to interfere with
> the required high-relief of the action and emotions.

One more problem, censorship, inhibited writers of ability and integrity who might wish to write for the stage. John Galsworthy, anxious to submit statements from famous men of letters to Lord Plymouth, directing a Joint Committee of Lords and Commons investigating problems related to censorship of plays, asked Hardy to prepare a letter useable in his cause. Hardy's letter, printed in *The Times* (13 August 1909), began briskly with the notation that writers 'who have other channels for communicating with the public' were probably deterred from writing for the stage by 'something or other – which probably is consciousness of the Censor'; and then went on to weigh in with his ounce of experience ('worth a ton of theory'). He noted that his ballad, 'A Sunday Morning Tragedy', published in the *English Review* in December 1908, had dealt with 'the fear of transgressing convention' overruling 'natural feeling to the extent of bringing dire disaster'; that this had seemed to him to be 'an eminently proper and moral subject' (he was, of course, indulging in irony); and that, for the sake of its inherent dramatic properties, it might well be produced as a tragic play. He had even gone so far 'as to shape the scenes, action, etc.' Realising at that point that he would never be able to get it on the boards, he then 'abandoned' the project. Hardy might well have added that even in its ballad form the poem had been rejected by the *Fortnightly* on the grounds that the review circulated amongst young people. As he wrote to Ford Madox Hueffer (Ford), editor of the *English Review*,

> Of course, with a larger morality, the guardians of young people would see that it is the very thing they ought to read, for nobody can say that the treatment is other than moral, and the crime is one of growing prevalence, as you probably know, and the false shame which leads to it is produced by the hypocrisy of the age.

The powerful spell cast by mummers had affected Hardy much earlier than the 1880s, however, and it is difficult to forget the scene in *The Return of the Native* (Eustacia acting as one of the mummers) that concludes with the cutting-off of the Saracen's head and the emergence of Saint George as victor:

> Nobody commented, any more than they would have commented on the fact of mushrooms coming in autumn or snow-drops in spring. They took the piece as phlegmatically as did the actors themselves. It was a phase of cheerfulness which was, as a matter of course, to be passed through every Christmas; and there was no more to be said.
>   They sang the plaintive chant which follows the play, during which all the dead men rose to their feet in a silent and awful manner, like the ghosts of Napoleon's soldiers in the Midnight Review. . . . (II, iv, v)

But *The Return of the Native*, incorporating as it does a rattling-quick version of the *Play of Saint George*, is more concerned with the play's narrative-line (and the developing characterisation of Eustacia) than with its mode of performance; and over the years Hardy, who apparently loved all aspects of mumming, had ample opportunity to review the reasons why the play had survived so many generations of Dorset life. 'On Christmas night [1920],' the *Life* records, 'the carol singers and mummers came to Max Gate as they had promised, the latter performing the *Play of Saint George*, just as he had seen it performed in his childhood.'[3] That very year, in the fall, he had prepared a recension of the mummers' play that might be used in Act II, Scene ii, of the Hardy Players' production of T. H. Tilley's version of *The Return of the Native*; and the actors who performed for Hardy in his drawing-room on that Christmas night were speaking the lines that Hardy, drawing upon his memories and earlier versions, had written for them. (The recension, published separately in 1921 and reprinted in New York in 1928, had wide circulation.)

It will be recalled that the Preface to *The Dynasts*, written in September 1903, referred to 'the technicalities of practical mumming'. Hardy, sufficiently concerned over the controversy that the unconventional form of his work had stirred up to invent the term 'epic-drama', was seeking some way of liberating his work from 'the material possibilities of stagery', to dispense with the theatre 'altogether'. He concluded his Preface with a striking suggestion of a new form of dramatic presentation, one that he would carry forward to its logical implementation in *The Queen of Cornwall* some two decades later:

> In respect of such plays of poesy and dream a practicable compromise may conceivably result, taking the shape of a monotonic delivery of speeches, with dreamy conventional gestures, something in the manner traditionally maintained by the old Christmas mummers, the curiously hypnotizing impressiveness of whose automatic style – that of persons who spoke by no will of their own – may be remembered by all who ever experienced it. Gauzes or screens to blur outlines might still further shut off the actual. . . .

One further aspect of staging concerned Hardy: he needed a name for his 'conventional onlooker', and thought that the word 'Chorus' carried un-English associations. (He conceded, in a letter to Harold Child, that 'they play the part of a Greek Chorus to some extent.')[4] As more suitable terms he introduced the name 'Chanters' and 'Ghosts', and these are identified, in the list of characters, as 'Shades of Dead Old Cornish Men' and 'Shades of Dead Cornish Women'.

It may all be a bit too much for an audience's pleasure: contempt for the mechanisms of theatre which intensify illusion; anti-representational fervour that demands more than ordinary co-operation from a spectator who must imagine greatly; murky lighting (the play begins with 'a blue light' on Merlin, the first speaker, who is described as 'a phantasmal figure with a white wand'); and a 'monotonic delivery' by human as well as supernatural characters. But Hardy was not writing conventional verse drama either, and his act of defiance against late Victorian theatre is not domesticated by any references we might make to what Shelley, Talfourd, and Browning had written a century earlier. Those poet-dramatists had wanted to succeed commercially, but they had been ignorant of theatrical realities, or too indolent to learn what actor-managers like Macready really needed. Hardy's knowledge of the theatre was considerable – I will measure its dimensions in a moment – but toward the end of his life, after reasoned consideration of what he could do best, and perhaps as important, what he wanted to do most, he was cutting free from all kinds of orthodoxy in *The Queen of Cornwall*, and, although the play is too short to explore fully its own possibilities as drama, and aspects of Hardy's experimentation will displease most playgoers, it was conceived in daring and original terms.

The play, for one thing, is a dream, conjured up by Merlin for the edification of his audience:

> I come, at your persuasive call,
> To raise up in this modern hall
> A tragedy of dire duresse
> That vexed the land of Lyonnesse: –
> Scenes, with their passions, hopes, and fears
> Sunk into shade these thousand years;
> To set, in ghostly grave array,
>   Their blitheness, blood, and tears,
> Feats, ardours, as if rife to-day
>   Before men's eyes and ears. . . .

The insistence on illusion is repeated in Merlin's Epilogue:

> These warriors and dear women, whom
> I've called, as bidden, from the tomb. . . .

It is deliberate distancing of the audience from the events recounted; in our fashionable cant, a knowing alienation. Dreaminess of gesture, chanting of lines, and even the hostile-tinged notation of Merlin ('Their mirth, crimes, fear and love begat / Your own, though thwart their ways. . . .') were all designed, from the beginning, to repel an audience's willingness to identify with the sufferers of the play's action. And although Hardy had no intention of reproducing the 'barbaric manners and

surroundings' of life as it really had been lived by contemporaries of King
Mark and Sir Tristram, and even called such historical verisimilitude
'impossible', he was determined not to follow the examples of Victorian
poets who had treated earlier eras: 'I have tried to avoid turning the rude
personages of, say, the fifth century into respectable Victorians, as was
done by Tennyson, Swinburne, Arnold, etc.' His characters were not
recognisably men and women of the modern world. Hardy also reached
beyond his customary limits by paying special attention to the unities.
Not that the notion of the perfect correspondence between stage time and
real time was novel by the end of the nineteenth century (the one-to-one
relationship in *The Queen of Cornwall* was perfected by an unbroken continuation of events and an absolute ban on scene-changing); such devices
had been used by many dramatists (including Ibsen) who had long since
become aware of the value of building tension and the sense of inevitability through scene after scene, all of which observed the unities. But
Hardy had tried only once to keep his background permanently fixed, in
The Return of the Native, and he was aware of the novelty of his effort, at
least in so far as his own practice was concerned.

The freedom with which he adapted his sources – for example, his
carefully marked copy of Ernest Rhys' edition of Malory, and probably
the versions of Joseph Bedier, Richard Wagner, and A. C. Swinburne, for
they were readily accessible to him as well – might well have been expected. Hardy could not have been worried over possible censures that he
had pulled together 'into the space of an hour events that in the traditional stories covered a long time'. Yet talk about unities and a Chorus
should remind us that Hardy's model was Greek drama more than any
other literary precedent, and indeed Hardy cited as justification for his
free-ranging use of source-materials the example of the Greek dramatists.

Hardy's relationship to Emma was conjured from the past, much as
Merlin's vision had been, and marked in a dedication: 'In affectionate
remembrance of those with whom I formerly spent many hours at the
scene of the tradition, who have now all passed away save one.' These
words were followed by the initials not only of Emma but of her sister
Helen Catherine Holder and of the man she had married, Caddell
Holder, the rector of St Juliot, as well as of his second wife Florence (who,
of course, was the surviving member of the quartet). It is the only dedication in all of Hardy's works. Some speculation has already stirred as to
whether the central dilemma of the play – Iseult the Fair, Queen of
Cornwall, and Iseult the Whitehanded, of Brittany, competing with each
other for the love of Tristram, and Tristram unable to choose freely

because he is no less a creature of destiny than they – echoes a moment of time when Hardy, not yet free from his engagement to Tryphena Sparks, met and visited Emma in Cornwall, where indeed he fell in love (1870–1872). But it is not necessary, or even desirable, to seek so close a correspondence. Such a reading inevitably casts Emma as the Queen of Cornwall, whose upbraidings of Tristram are both shrewish and harrowing, and unfairly calls into question the sincerity of the dedication ('affectionate remembrance'). Further evidence that he was paying respectful homage to Emma (if such evidence is needed) may be found in the 'Imaginary View of Tintagel Castle' that he used as frontispiece for the published edition of the play. The picture was based on one of Emma's watercolours, and finished with earnest and meticulous detail by Hardy. Moreover, Tristram's fumbled responses to the Queen's complaints sketch a portrait of irresolution and final failure. Neither in the early 1870s nor in 1923 did Hardy see himself in these terms.

Yet the play, in addition to its value as a statement of theatrical philosophy, of the relationship between form and function, resonates with a personal note. Perhaps not surprisingly: Hardy, in a letter to Alfred Noyes (17 November 1923), spoke of it as having been '53 years in contemplation'. He would not have written it if the Tristram legend had not been closely associated with the 'various picturesque points' of Cornwall, which (in the Preface to *A Pair of Blue Eyes*) he had called 'the region of dream and mystery'. And, as already noted, he had visualised Emma as an incarnated Iseult. If biographical parallels are not pursued with a frightening literalism, we can readily agree that any play written about Cornwall and a fated love affair would become a personal document.

Ultimately, however, *The Queen of Cornwall* must be judged as drama, and not as the opera that Rutland Boughton a few years later adapted in collaboration with Hardy. Many Englishmen are familiar only with Boughton's version, which may have received more productions than Hardy's original: the score enlarged the text (Hardy wanted 'to bring it roughly to the average length of Greek plays'); examples of the rethinking of the action are notable in Scene XIII, which now became three scenes; in the deletion of the Prologue and the Epilogue; and in the addition of half a dozen lyrics from earlier volumes of verse written by Hardy. What Boughton did for the sake of intensifying a series of moods had an expectable (if subtle) distorting effect; and Hardy, who watched a performance of Boughton's version at Glastonbury, observed justly, but without resentment, that the opera shifted the sympathies of the audience from Iseult the Whitehanded, where he had meant them to be directed, to the Queen of Cornwall.

Hardy's play, though a minor work within his own canon, is not only a reading experience of genuine merit, but viable theatre. The emphasis upon the workings of the love-potion, drunk long before the catastrophe of this particular moment of action, provides the audience with the same kind of superior knowledge that Greek audiences must have had when watching enacted myths. Nothing that the Queen of Cornwall can say in her beratings, or Tristram can offer in extenuation of his unforgivable behaviour, will change the relationships. As the Shades of the Dead Cornish Women say, these figures are 'in love Fate-haunted', and the 'charmed philtres' have melted 'every link of purposed faith'. To the 'forebodings' of Queen Iseult, to the knowledge that 'darkness over-draws us', Tristram can only respond by playing a prelude on the harp:

> Yea, Love, true is it sadness suits me best;
> Sad, sad we are; sad, sad shall ever be. . . .

Tristram's defence – that he never sinned willingly; that all wrong committed against the Queen of Cornwall was done 'under sorcery unwittingly', and through the agency of a 'love-compelling vial' – is obviously inadequate, and offered in a death-speech (after Mark has stabbed him in the back). And the final speech of Iseult the Whitehanded repeats what we already know, bone-deep:

> . . . even had I not come
> Across the southern water recklessly
> This would have shaped the same – the very same.

Pity may be the emotion Hardy intended to evoke; pity is what we surely feel for Iseult the Whitehanded, who, as J. O. Bailey notes,[5] has sinned the least; but as in any reworking of familiar materials, the play provides some original variations beyond the dark previsionings that finally turn true and leave a shattered Iseult the Whitehanded moaning softly to herself.

> Aye, I will rise –
> Betake me to my own dear Brittany –
> Dearer in that our days there were so sweet,
> Before I knew what pended me elsewhere!

Hardy has consistently characterised her position as hopeless, from the moment that she enters (she has 'corn-brown hair', a significant detail), and Sir Andret describes her as 'feather-shaken / Like a far bird stray-blown.' She pleads with Tristram, begging forgiveness: 'I could not help it, O my husband!' But she is an innocent, striving to cope with a situation beyond her control, and when Tristram rebuffs her, 'she breaks down', confesses that she is 'tired, / Tired, tired', that her 'once-dear Brittany home' has become a desert to her; and faints.

This is an original reading of the character of Iseult the Whitehanded. Also unexpected, though a minor touch, is the appearance of a humble damsel with a letter (xx). The dialogue of thrust-and-parry between the Queen of Cornwall and Tristram, expressing a bitterness that can find no amelioration given the circumstances of Tristram's return to Lyonnesse, is underscored by Hardy's adaptation of similar acrid exchanges in *A Pair of Blue Eyes*, a novel completed a full half-century before,[6] and becomes a distinct contribution to the legend as found. Finally, as one additional surprising element, the manner of King Mark's death: the Queen of Cornwall 'snatches King Mark's dagger from his belt and stabs him with it', and exults:

> Thus. Done! My last deed – save my very last –
> To null myself, as if I never had been . . .
> – I have lived! I have loved! O I have loved indeed. . . .

An unanticipated stage-direction follows (perhaps all the more specta-cular because of the bareness of the stage):

> A few moments' pause during which the sea and sky darken yet
> more, and the wind rises, distant thunder murmuring. Torches
> are moving about in the shadows at the back of the scene. . . .

A poet's touch, but the entire play is poetically conceived. The moments of verbal felicity – as in Queen Iseult's song, 'Could he but live for me' (vii), and Tristram's song, 'Let's meet again to-night, my Fair' (xi) – are set firmly within a context: a darkly-imaged world for whose inhabitants happiness is illusory, and for whom death becomes the final liberation.

7

Hardy's Views on Christianity

A man's relationship to his God, however private he may wish it to remain, invites scrutiny if it becomes the subject-matter of his art. The autobiographical substratum of much of Hardy's verse – what Hardy called the 'personal particulars' of his life – is inescapable, partly because Hardy claimed for himself the privilege of recording in verse views that he did not choose to express in novels, and partly because Hardy believed that his controversial views would excite fewer of the 'literary contortionists' who had attacked the appearance of each new novel. 'If Galileo had said in verse that the world moved, the Inquisition might have let him alone', he wrote dryly on 17 October 1896, at about the time he was renouncing the craft of novel-writing.[1] His concern with the formal Christianity he did not intellectually believe in became even more marked in his creative efforts after that date; poems seeking to define the grounds of a true Christian's faith in an increasingly non-Christian world may be found in every volume of verse that he published.

I believe in the sincerity and truth of the remark, dictated by an ailing Hardy to his second wife, and already quoted once, that 'there is more autobiography in a hundred lines of Mr. Hardy's poetry than in all the novels.'[2] In my analysis, due credit will be given to the art, whether 'dramatic or impersonative even where not explicitly so' (Preface to *Poems of the Past and the Present*), but an assumption to keep in mind throughout is that Hardy, shaken in his faith by theological arguments, reading, and independent thinking by the time he reached his early twenties, did not 'repent' on his deathbed.[3] A second cautionary note is that Hardy did not swiftly or dramatically change his views. The verse of his final years, when dealing with aspects of Christianity, may best be characterised as self-convinced, humanely sceptical, and occasionally tinged by genuine regret; these terms may equally well be applied to many earlier efforts; but a genuine change *did* take place in the final years.

Yet, before we move to the examination of specific poems, we should recall the intense interest with which Hardy watched and encouraged the efforts of the Church of England in the 1920s to revise its liturgy, to minimise the supernatural element, and to gather 'many millions of waiting agnostics into its fold'.[4] He knew of no other 'purely English establishment' that had comparable 'dignity and footing, with such strength of old association, such scope for transmutability, such architectural spell', that could 'keep the shreds of morality together'. Hardy noted that he himself had never been called 'churchy', though he thought the term more appropriate than many that had been applied, and he added,

> . . . not in an intellectual sense, but in so far as instincts and emotions ruled. As a child, to be a parson had been his dream; moreover, he had had several clerical relatives who held livings; while his grandfather, father, uncle, brother, wife, cousin, and two sisters had been musicians in various churches over a period covering altogether more than a hundred years. He himself had frequently read the church lessons, and had at one time as a young man begun reading for Cambridge with a view to taking Orders.[5]

The final moment in a series of moments of disenchantment came when *The Book of Common Prayer* appeared in new form, with what Hardy called its 'preternatural assumptions' still retained.

Hardy, arriving in London at the age of twenty-one (he had been a child of approximately eight the first time he saw the metropolis), carried two necessary letters of introduction, the Bible, and the *Book of Common Prayer*; both books had been given to him by his parents. These he marked with pencilled references to events – those taking place between 1859 and 1897 in the Bible, and those of 1919 in the Prayer Book.[6] But what a younger man might need in the way of spiritual solace inevitably changed. A conviction that miracles lessened rather than enhanced scriptural authority became firm. 'Panthera', the poem which postulated the existence of a Roman soldier as the father of Jesus (a legend borrowed from Haeckel and Strauss), was part of a determined effort by Hardy to remove the myth from the rationally acceptable life-story of Christ, an effort that he made in common with other distinguished Victorians like Matthew Arnold, in order to save the Christian religion from decline. One of the most telling poems of *Winter Words*, 'An Evening in Galilee', is cast in the form of a monologue by Mary, who wonders whether her son is mad; she makes no reference to any of his miracles that he is supposed to have wrought; she does not believe as he does ('He professes as his firm faiths things far too grotesque to be true. . . .'), but he is a preacher, an expounder, a reader of unfamiliar philosophies, rather than a transformer into loaves and fishes, a healer who raises men from the dead, or a walker upon the water. Mary anticipates the 'tragedy-brink' of her son's life, the likelihood of his 'arrest, and death', but she does not know how to warn Joseph. Moreover, reacting with understandable bitterness to Jesus's denial of her relationship to him ('Who is my mother?'), she poses the far more troublesome question, 'Who is my father?' The answer to that is known by Joseph, herself, 'and – one other', who will never see her again; what happened between herself and that 'other' is attributed to a chance encounter, she 'dreaming no ill', at the time it happened; in all likelihood Hardy alluded, however indirectly, to the Panthera legend. Mary is thus characterised as an artless, baffled, unhappy mother, incapable of perceiving the full meaning of either her son's preachings or his associations with 'the lowest folk' (fishermen, Mary Magdalene); most important, she is wholly human, and she thinks of Jesus as explainable, for all his erratic behaviour, without recourse to the imagery of supernatural agencies.

Hardy's attitude toward the suspension of natural laws is consistent. 'In the Servants' Quarters', a modernised rendering of the triple denial of Peter's relationship to Jesus, ends with the crowing of the morning cock. The poet follows the Gospels with sympathetic and imaginative fidelity, but the serviceable, homely realism of the exchanges between the servants, the constables, and Peter does not state, or even imply, that Peter is convinced of the divinity of Jesus, who is referred to not as the Redeemer but as a 'criminal', a man being brought to judgement for blasphemies. 'A Drizzling Easter Morning' begins with the rhetorical question, 'And he is risen?', before it continues to point out, with more than a touch of melancholia, that 'dead men wait as long ago', and – if consulted – may not wish to rise again; they certainly do not rise again so far as the poet can tell. 'I stand amid them in the rain', he writes, and the old pattern of work ('the weary wain' and 'toilers with their aches') continues for ever; those who live look forward to 'endless rest'. The point of the poem is that for them, no less than for those who are already in the grave, it makes no difference whether Jesus is risen. Jesus is said to have lived 'an innocent life' in 'The Clasped Skeletons', a poem written to commemorate the excavation of 'an Ancient British barrow near the writer's house', and Procula, Pilate's wife, does not weep for the son of God but for a man unjustly condemned. Indeed, in the series of rounds that constitutes 'Drinking Song', the history of civilisation seems to turn out to be a number of speculations as to the nature of man – by Thales, Copernicus, Hume, Darwin, Thomas Kelly Cheyne, and Einstein – none of which is definitive, yet all of which offer respectable versions of reality for a given age. These great thoughts include the notion that miracles are unnecessary, and the rationalist's argument that Mary was not a virgin when she bore Jesus. 'Such tale, indeed,' Cheyne is made to say in his capacity as a scholar of Biblical texts, 'helps not our creed', and is 'a tale long known to none'.

Hardy's emphasis on the *naturalness* of religion should not be construed as being in any sense an attack on the emotional core of Christianity, for he regarded religion as necessary: it 'must be retained unless the world is to perish', he wrote in the 'Apology' to *Late Lyrics and Earlier*. What he wanted was Christianity to earn the right to renewed credibility among those who had fled, in dismay, from many of its supernatural assertions. These, in turn, defied 'complete rationality' and boggled the imagination. But he became increasingly uncertain that the formal Church institutions of his age, besieged by textual disintegrators, scientific reorganisers of the sum of the world's knowledge, and the men of the cloth disinclined to change, would ever benefit from 'the interfusing effect of poetry', from what Wordsworth, in his Preface to the Second Edition of *Lyrical Ballads*, defined as 'the breath and finer spirit of all knowledge; . . . the impassioned expression which is in the countenance of all Science.'

The dilemma of Christianity is even more complex than that, however. Hardy informs us that the faith of Jesus – as distinct from the life-story, now hopelessly shrouded with story-telling inventions and fabulous artifices – has been systematised and transmogrified into something quite different from what Jesus believed it to be. 'In St. Paul's a While Ago', a soliloquy by Hardy that may have been composed as early as 1869 but was first printed in *Human Shows*, Paul is characterised as 'that strange Jew, Damascus-bound', with a

> vision-seeing mind
> Charmless, blank in every kind,

whose 'eager, stammering speech' would have been dismissed by Hardy's contemporaries, had they been able to hear it, as the message of 'an epilept enthusiast'. The problem of learning what Christ had to tell us is twice compounded: first, by Paul's intoxicated visions (the 'drifts of gray illumination' that Hardy sees spilling down 'from the lofty fenestration' of the English cathedral are symbolically fitting, for the joy of Jesus is not to be found within 'chilly Paul's, / With its chasmal classic walls'), and second, by the trivial interests of the modern age, as exemplified by statues of 'cadaverous' and 'wan' visage and by visitors to the cathedral; the latter are 'all unknowing or forgetting' of the real Paul, and are given secularised names:

> A brimming Hebe, rapt in her adorning,
> Brushes an Artemisia craped in mourning:
> Beatrice Benedick piques, coquetting; . . .

In 'Winter Night in Woodland', Hardy contrasts the fox-hunters, bird-baiters, poachers, smugglers, and drunken stay-at-homes against the Mellstock singers 'just afoot on their long yearly rounds', who have set out 'to rouse by worn carols each house in their bounds'. Robert Penny, the Dewys, Mail, Voss, and the rest represent an age that had vanished even before Hardy's birth; the Mellstock quire (as in *Under the Greenwood Tree*) symbolises an earlier and more innocent time. Hardy's first three stanzas present us with illegal and even brutal and murderous behaviour that in no way has been checked by the spirit of Christ's teaching, or modified by the meaning of 'the rhythm of voices and strings' carried through the countryside after midnight by the quire. Christ has had no effect on the perpetrators of these activities.

Thus, it is not clear that Christ's having lived and died has improved the lot of mankind beyond expanding the choices available to those who want to believe in a credible God. A poem that illustrates this view is 'Christmas in the Elgin Room', begun (presumably) while Hardy was conducting research in the British Museum for *The Dynasts*, and completed very close to the end of his life (the dates appended to the poem are 1905 and 1926). Hardy imagines, in a characteristic irony of juxtaposed attitudes, what the Greek gods represented in the Elgin marbles ('those whom Christmas overthrew') might say about the pealing of Christmas bells. The Nativity which the occasion celebrates – according to those gods – was

> said to have been a day of cheer,
> And source of grace
> To the human race. . . .

But the fate of the Elgin marbles – to have been sold 'for Borean people's gold' and brought to London – was grimmer for more than the simple reason that England is the land of the 'Borean people', or even their recognition that the British Museum houses them in an unworthy and demeaning 'gaunt room / Which sunlight shuns'. Remembering where they had been, 'on Athenai's Hill', they sigh for the better times they have known: 'Before this Christ was known, and we had men's good will.' Hardy juxtaposes the pagan past and the Christian present, but not for cheaply ironic effect as, easily enough perhaps, he might have done. He is not, for example, suggesting that the 'deities fair' whom Pheidias sculpted represented a truer concept of religion than than which has replaced them. They have had their day; 'old Helios', 'the Ilissus River-god', Demeter, Poseidon, Persephone, and all the others are remembered today only because an Englishman brought them from their ignominious repose (as broken limbs and 'shards beneath some Acropolitan clod') to a land where restoration had at least indicated a measure of their value to those who cared for their memories as the powerful gods they once had been.

Hardy's note is more subtle and, correspondingly, more disturbing. The yesteryear when the Greek gods were 'radiant' will never come again; that he knows, and concedes. But the Christianity of the modern world, for all the sound of bells – variously described as shaking the night, clanging, and singing – is not presented as a cheerful condition of life either. Hardy could have suggested as much by allowing the gods to speculate on whether the significance of the Nativity had been truly understood; if men were acting on the basis of the meaning of the allegory that Christ's life provided. Even when we grant the limitations of perspective (the Greek gods, those 'of Zeus' high breed', cannot know for certain what is happening in the outer world), the poem provides no evidence that the new faith is 'radiant' – based on mutual confidence between the people and the gods they worship – or serene. The gods are in exile, and a gloomy one it has proved to be; they cannot be sure that the sun of Christ is any warmer than the 'Aurore' that 'but enters cold' their museum windows. Their ignorance may well be Hardy's uncertainty: how warming is the Christian faith to men of the twentieth century?

'Christmas: 1924', a quatrain, notes the ambiguity of the 'advances' of civilisation. These have brought to us, and to Hardy only three years before his death, the perfection of a new weapon of mass destruction, poison-gas. But it is difficult to tell if Hardy laments here the tattering of the dreams of the League of Nations more or less than he laments the futility of the message preached by 'a million priests', the invocation of 'Peace upon earth!' which apparently means little or nothing to the modern world.

There is, however, no shading of ambiguity in the poem 'Unkept Good Fridays', which Hardy dated 'Good Friday, 1927'. It is a surprisingly powerful statement for a poem written so close to the end; the passion of the poem still has the power to move us more than a half-century later. Hardy believed that Christ's goodness (his human virtues?) had led to envy, betrayal, and death; but this kind of sacrifice had not been unique in the annals of man.

> There are many more Good Fridays
> Than this, if we but knew
> The names . . .

The sacrificial victims, the 'nameless Christs', will remain for ever un-counted because their agonies have been unpenned. Such is the drift of four of the five stanzas, which essentially repeat the commonality of the fate of other martyrs; they were slain for their 'goodwill' by the rulers and the mobs who tortured, smote, and trampled them under into unmarked graves, on unscored dates.

If Hardy had concluded with the fourth stanza, the poem might have remained a conventionalised and unsurprising statement of Christian doctrine: the good man is fated to be scorned, to live through 'days of bonds and burning', there are many Christs, and their Good Fridays will never be commemorated. But the fifth stanza goes much further, and argues that the failure to remember who they were really doesn't matter:

> The world was not even worthy
> To taunt their hopes and aims . . .

We have not been worthy of them or of Jesus. We have already dis-honoured the memory of the Christ we knew. Why, then, should we assume that we could or would honour the memory of any of the name-less Christs – 'these Christs of unwrit names' – if in fact we were to be informed of the nobility of their individual moments on Calvary? The final message of Hardy's poem is best characterised as bleak. Christ was, and remains today, too good for us. We rejected him, and all who followed in his footsteps, and we are where we are today because our Christianity is hollow. 'Good Friday, 1927' can thus be read as a final comment on 'Christmas in the Elgin Room'. The old gods are exiled, imprisoned in the British Museum, devitalised; but the god of Christian-ity, the true and living Christ, may never have been believed in, and even worse, it is not in human nature – as the New Dark Age moves in, engulfing us – to understand and appreciate the meaning of Good Friday.

Now all of this goes beyond many of the critical commentaries on Hardy's concept of Immanent Will, which place so much emphasis on the mocking detachment of the Spirits, particularly in *The Dynasts*, where the meaning of the Will is most fully expounded and interpreted. It will be recalled that several of the Spirits are denominated as pitying, as sinister, as ironic; with one or two minor exceptions they do not participate in the action of the fated decade between 1805 and 1815; they remain far above the action; and the Immanent Will never speaks for itself anyhow. It has been easy to assume that Hardy identifies with his Spirits, and has adopted a pose of superiority to the agonies of mankind, the 'shapes that bleed, mere mannikins', each of which 'has parcel in the total Will'. At any rate, the temptation has not been consistently resisted.

But it may be questioned whether, in his final decade, Hardy's perception of a failed faith was impersonally rendered in such poems as we have been considering, or whether Hardy, like the Ezekiel whose Book he had been reading on at least one Good Friday, responded to the barbarities of his age with increasing concern and a sense of deepening personal involvement. Those familiar with the magnificent speech of the Chorus of the Years at Waterloo remember how the poet imagined the war as seen from the height and perspective of the small animals and birds on that bloody battlefield; but equally poignant was the speech that followed, uttered by the Chorus of the Pities:

> So the season's intent, ere its fruit unfold,
> Is frustrate, and mangled, and made succumb,
> Like a youth of promise struck stark and cold!
>
> (III.VI.viii)

Hardy's unhappiness over the broken promises of the Christian religion is closely related to his conviction that the Church of England in the 1920s could not respond to felt needs, to his perception of the vastness of the gulf between institutionalised worship and the intellectual like himself who wanted to return to a simpler faith, and to his concern that the human race as a whole had already denied the possibility of its redemption; like Peter in 'In the Servants' Quarters', we had known the Christ and refused to acknowledge him.

> 'No! I'll be damned in hell if I know anything about the man!
> No single thing about him more than everybody knows!
> Must not I even warm my hands but I am charged with
>   blasphemies?'

It is true Hardy denied that he spoke directly in his poems. He expressed frequently his willingness to believe that critics read 'meanings into a book that its author never dreamt of writing there'. In his final tart comment on 'licensed tasters', contained in his Preface to *Winter Words*, he wrote that their odd verdicts arose not from wilful misrepresentation but from a failure to read what he had written. Still, it would be strange if Hardy did not occasionally – in poems on a topic so close to his heart as

the Christian faith and the difficulties that he stumbled over as he sought
to partake of its blessings – sound an unmistakable personal note. In two
poems particularly he described his private feelings at what should be the
most joyous season of the year: 'Christmastide' and 'A Nightmare, and
the next Thing'. In the former Hardy contrasts his own mood, as he
strides 'despondently' through the rain, with the mood of a poor man
headed toward the Casuals' Gate of the Union House, where he will be
fed and housed for the night; the tramp, too, is sodden, but he has not
lost his cheer, and the poem ends abruptly, without any indication that
the tramp's shouted salutation, 'A merry Christmas, friend!', has improved the spirits of the poet.

In the latter poem, again, the contrast is deliberately set: on the one
hand the poet, depressed by the 'fogged and blurred' empty street of a
'nightmare Christmas Day'; and, on the other, 'three clammy casuals'
headed toward the Union House, laughing, alive, and unaware of any
reason why they should share the poet's melancholia. No one else, in
fact, sees the 'gray nightmare / Astride the day, or anywhere'. Is 'the next
thing' of the title Death itself, as J. O. Bailey surmises?[7] If so, the depressed
mood of the poem must be tied closely to old age, debilitation, fragile
health. Yet only the presence of the poem in Hardy's last volume suggests lateness of composition (it is undated, as indeed are many of the
poems we would like to know more about). Without speculating on the
relationship of 'A Nightmare, and the Next Thing' to Hardy's conviction,
in his late eighties, that he had outstayed his welcome, we may still
observe that both poems present Christmas as a personally gloomy
experience. Hardy does not deny that others may feel invigorated by the
season; the poet, the 'I' of each poem, is plunged deeply into a mood that
Christ's birth seems powerless to lighten.[8]

Hardy's final poems are sadder and more measured in pace. They turn
backward to earlier and happier times; it is only natural that thoughts of
Christmas in the post-war world should suffer by comparison with
thoughts of Christmas enjoyed while a child. In 'Yuletide in a Younger
World', for example, Hardy recalls, from his own boyhood, 'doings of
delight', speculations on phantoms crossing a 'bridge or stile', the craft of
divination to 'read men's dreams. . . / Even as wheels spin round', and a
sense of closeness to 'the fartime tones of fire-filled prophets / Long on
earth unseen. . . .' But these have long since gone: 'Now we are blinker-
bound.' There is a finality to this recognition. Not only have the happy
events and innocent beliefs of childhood receded into a remote past for
the poet, but the possibility of ever reclaiming them is now seen as hopeless. Nor is his recollection of those moments of pleasure afforded the

innocent eye spoiled by the wisdom of his eighty-sixth birthday ('He Never Expected Much'), which suggests that life, from the very beginning, warned him that he would experience 'just neutral-tinted haps and such', that the World would not all be fair. Most ageing poets would understand Hardy's mood of steely-edged nostalgia, and do.

Preparation for a final reckoning informs many of the poems in Hardy's last volumes of verse, and those with religious content seem peculiarly final in their point of view. I find particularly poignant 'Sine Prole', that Hardy wrote in deliberate imitation of a medieval Latin sequence by Adam of S. Victor, for here Hardy faced the certainty that he would have no descendants, children or grandchildren, because his family tree had run out:

> To the moment where I stand
> Has my line wound: I the last one –

and even if Hardy's view of post-war Europe was to harden a conviction that no child could or would grow to manhood cheered by the prospects of an eternally barbarous mankind, the thought of dying childless was inevitably grim.

Human Shows is rich in these penultimate musings, which suggest that the nature of the Immanent Will had long since been settled to the poet's satisfaction, and that other questions now crowded front and centre. In 'The Graveyard of Dead Creeds', for example, Hardy treated all the religions of the past as 'old wastes of thought' which had outlived their usefulness, 'Catholicons' or cure-alls that no longer might solace 'created man, through his long groan'. Hardy did not consider it necessary to identify the 'heir' who would bring 'new promise' to the world, who would, in the words of the spectres of the 'dead creeds',

> 'make tolerable to sentient seers
> The melancholy marching of the years.'

The nature of that heir had been defined elsewhere; in his 'Apology' affixed to *Late Lyrics and Earlier*; in the hints about the self-conscious awakening of the Will in the After Scene of *The Dynasts*, as well as in a number of the Spirits' comments earlier; and in an extended passage written during January 1907, and later incorporated into the *Life*, where he spoke of the need for a non-magical, non-superstitious religion that thinking men might respect. Perhaps Hardy underestimated the difficulties that such a religion might pose for the great mass of his fellow-countrymen, and he surely did not want to be considered an original – and hence controversial – speculator on theological doctrine. But there are more than passing traces of regret in his comments on the value of ceremony and liturgy, even while, at the same time, he admitted to being unhappy with the twentieth-century stress on the morality and altruism of Jesus ('an entirely different meaning from that which it bore when I was a boy'). The meaning of Christianity had been altered, refracted, by the Higher Criticism, which he regarded as the unpleasant opposing extreme of the mysticism against which it had reacted; but how was 'Sinceritas' – 'the Would-be-Religious' – to define the middle ground?

Hardy took keen interest in the possibility that a comparative study of religions might answer the questions that interpreters of Christianity avoided in their insistence on dogma or on their disintegrative analysis of texts. Toward the end of his life he quoted in his *Notebooks* a sentence used by the Oxford Dictionary to illustrate the meaning of sentience, quoted from FitzEdward Hall's *Hindu Philosophical System* (1862): 'The Sankhyas use them [the works of God] to prove that the whole world, every consti-tuent part of which is for an end, has for its author that which possesses no sentience – nature.'[9] He read widely in 'other moral religions within whose sphere the name of Christ has never been heard', and which taught the same doctrine 'of nobler feelings towards humanity and emotional goodness and greatness'.[10] He made notes on psychic pheno-mena, worried over the possible relevance of Einstein's doctrine of relativity, read with some scepticism Worsley's *Concepts of Monism,* and gave full credit to the significance of Comte's 'Positive Religion'. The usability of various philosophical works – by Mill, Stephen, Spencer probably more than by others – has been defined in a long chapter, 'Impressions of Reality', in Walter Wright's *The Shaping of 'The Dynasts': A Study in Thomas Hardy* (1967), and the whole matter of Hardy's eclecticism in both philo-sophical and religious readings is best summarised by Wright's sentence, 'We must keep in mind that Hardy wavered between alternatives in his search for a cosmic view' (p. 53), which suggests that Hardy retained reservations about all men's systems; that ultimately institutionalised religion, as he saw it, was a human construct, and could not help but be vulnerable to examination and questioning, as any human construct must be.

There is no way to measure the solace that Hardy derived from the limited and severely rationalised Christianity of the late nineteenth century. The poems offer dramatised versions of what are certainly conflicting – not necessarily 'developing' – points of view. Hardy believed that a writer was obligated only to write as well as he could what he knew and felt; the term 'pessimism' he regarded as an irrelevant criterion, one that might have been more appropriately applied to Gray's 'Ode on a

Distant Prospect of Eton College' than to his own poetry. 'Oh, Gray is an unbearable poet', he burst out while talking to Vere Collins (29 October 1921). '. . . I suppose "pessimism" is an easy word to say and remember. It's only a passing fashion.'[11] Yet his poems dealing with religion, those that articulate in some way the religious impulse, become increasingly melancholy in the final volumes, and are inseparably bound up with his sense of the unlikelihood that men could benefit from Christ's example. Writing to Sydney Cockerell on 28 August 1914, he mused, glumly, 'As for myself, the recognition that we are all living in a more brutal age than that, say, of Elizabeth, or of the chivalry which could cry: "Gentlemen of the Guard, fire first!" (far more brutal, indeed: no chivalry now!) does not inspire one to write hopeful poetry, or even conjectural prose, but simply makes one sit still in an apathy, and watch the clock spinning backwards, with a mild wonder if, when it gets back to the Dark Ages, and the sack of Rome, it will ever move forward again to a new Renascence, and a new literature.' He added hastily, 'But people would call this pessimistic, so I will stop. . . .'[12]

As a consequence, a critic's emphasis may fall on the hopelessness contained in the speeches of the wind ('A Night of Questionings'), which proclaim the unchanging evil of man's nature; human beings breathe 'dark-drawn breaths' and 'knave their neighbours' deaths', revert 'backward to type', and will never grow purer. Or it may identify, as more genuinely expressive of Hardy's longer-term belief, the hopefulness contained in such late poems as 'There Seemed a Strangeness' and 'Xenophanes, the Monist of Colophon', which look forward to the ultimate awakening of the Will, and the revelation of God's intentions:

> 'Men have not heard, men have not seen
> Since the beginning of the world
>   What earth and heaven mean;
> But now their curtains shall be furled,
>
> 'And they shall see what is, ere long,
> Not through a glass, but face to face;
> And Right shall disestablish Wrong: . . .'
>
> ('There Seemed a Strangeness')

But, over all, Hardy's views are more mordant than sanguine, and the possibility that the Will may never awaken from its complacent sleep is marked by quoted speeches (Hardy never says directly and personally that a 'Great Adjustment' will take place; he has a vision in which 'vermilion light' floods 'the land's lean face', he hears 'a Voice', – these things seem to be and cannot be said actually to be), by the rumblings in letters and comments preserved by visitors to Max Gate, by a number of poems in which inclement weather becomes symbolic of defeated hopes for the triumph of loving-kindness.

It is not unreasonable, then, to end with a consideration of 'Evening Shadows', a poem in *Winter Words* that had appeared first in the *Daily Telegraph* on 7 May 1928. It was one of Hardy's final meditations on the religious impulse. Hardy muses on the relationship between pre-Christian burial mounds – in this case, Conquer Barrow, not far from his home – and the 'earthen cyst' in which some day he will lie buried himself. It is a convenient opportunity to platitudinise, to suggest, for example, that he will ultimately be forgotten just as the identity of the Britons who are covered by the barrow has long since been obliterated, or to point out that Christianity has not more claim to permanence than the dead creed of the pagan dead. Such, indeed, is part of the poem's message; but only part. He is not sure what will happen after his own death, whether the chimneys of Max Gate will continue to smoke and cast their shadows 'upon the greensward'. More important than his speculation that Conquer Barrow may still 'spread around' its shade many years hence – he does not know for a fact that it will – is his belief that now, in the last decade of his life, the Christian faith is as unregarded, as unbelieved in, as when Conquer Barrow itself was created:

> And nothing says such shade will spread around
> Even as to-day when men will no more heed
> The Gospel news than when the mound was made.

In brief, Hardy's final attitude seems to be this: in his own lifetime Christianity had lost its power to convert the would-be believer, and to cheer and comfort 'Sinceritas'. Thomas Hardy, grown poignantly old, thought of Christianity as a dying creed.

8

War and *Pax Britannica*

I have often thought that a diary-entry made by Thomas Hardy in the section dated 'August onwards' of 1914 is in several respects the most poignant, melancholy, and revealing passage of that thinly disguised autobiography, *Later Years*. The date marked the onset of the Great War, though nobody, not even Hardy, could have predicted its length or the full measure of its bloodiness; but the diary notation was also an extraordinary opportunity for Hardy – who acknowledged himself to be 'an old man of seventy-four' – to look back on a lifetime of thinking about the horrors of war. This chapter assesses the importance of that theme in Hardy's poetry – and might well begin with a review of the circumstances whereby Hardy, several years after the publication of Part III of *The Dynasts*, became a poet on war themes once again.

He had been invited by Mr Masterman, Chancellor of the Duchy of Lancaster, acting on behalf of the Cabinet, to Wellington House, Buckingham Gate, for a 'private Conference in which eminent literary men and women who commanded confidence abroad should "take steps to place the strength of the British case and the principles for which the British troops and their allies are fighting before the populations of neutral countries." ' Also present were Sir James Barrie, Sir Henry Newbolt, J. W. Mackail, Arthur and Monsignor Benson, John Galsworthy, Sir Owen Seaman, G. M. Trevelyan, H. G. Wells, Arnold Bennett, John Masefield, Robert Bridges, Anthony Hope Hawkins, Gilbert Murray, and many others. Hardy, speaking of himself (as usual) in the third person, continued:

> . . . Whatever the effect of the discussion, the scene was impressive to more than one of them there. In recalling it Hardy said that the yellow September sun shone in from the dusty street with a tragic cast upon them as they sat round the large blue table, full of misgivings, yet unforeseeing in all their completeness the tremendous events that were to follow. The same evening Hardy left London – 'the streets hot and sad, and bustling with soldiers and recruits' – to set about some contribution to the various forms of manifesto that had been discussed.

The Great War was to destroy all Hardy's belief in the gradual ennoble-ment of man; he himself confessed as much; he added, bleakly, 'He said he could probably not have ended *The Dynasts* as he did end it if he could have foreseen what was going to happen within a few years.' In this new view of the Universe, Consciousness would not (and could not) inform the Will, 'till It fashion all things fair', for Hardy could not longer cherish the hope, however thin, that somewhere there existed 'a fundamental ultimate Wisdom'.

My line of argument, in brief, is that Thomas Hardy, who so violently and so often reacted against charges that he was a pessimist in his art, finally became one in his study at Max Gate, and that he did so largely as a consequence of reflections on the 'barbaric age' in which men and women lived as 'the slaves of gross superstition'. The irony of this capitu-lation to his darkest fears, an event that took place a full decade before his death, is worth considering in detail. It has not often enough been noted. It may well have been the supreme irony in the life of a writer who understood well the 'little ironies' of human existence.

How did Hardy contribute to the war effort of 1914–18? In his public statements he appeared to be a convinced and committed patriot, from the writing of 'Men Who March Away', two days after the conference at Wellington House, to the last of the seventeen 'Poems of War and Patriotism' that formed a substantial section of *Moments of Vision* (1917). I will return to these poems later. For the moment let me say that they orchestrate old themes – Hardy's hatred of dynasts who provoke wars for their own aggrandisement, his compassion for the victims of war, his conviction that the peoples of Europe would recognise their fraternal bonds (which he believed to be stronger than their differences), his faith in the values of English life and the English countryside. He was active in a number of other ways: he encouraged Harley Granville-Barker's production of selected scenes from *The Dynasts*, undertaken as a re-minder to English audiences that the menace of Bonapartism had been defeated only a century before (Rebecca West, among others, was deeply moved by a performance), and he appreciated, in perhaps equal measure, the selection made by the Hardy Players of *Wessex Scenes from the Dynasts*.

Hardy visited the German prisoners of war in a camp at Dorchester, gave them 'food and medicines', and earned their respect as someone who believed in them 'as individuals'. Mrs Florence Hardy wrote to Sir Sydney Cockerell on 10 November 1916 to say, 'It is pleasant to know that those Germans were grateful, that they wrote to their families in Germany about him, and that a letter came back saying that as a result of his consideration the English prisoners in that part of Germany were receiving better treatment.'

He permitted wide reprinting of his war poems as a gift to the Allied cause; he did not, for example, reserve a copyright on 'Men Who March Away'. In a letter to the *Manchester Guardian* of 7 October 1914 he deplored the damage sustained by Rheims Cathedral, damage that could not be undone however faithful the restoration; the stained glass, he wrote, was 'inimitable by any handiworkers in the craft nowadays'; moreover, 'Gothic architecture has been a dead art for the last three hundred years, in spite of the imitations thrown broadcast over the land, and much of what is gone from the fine structure is gone forever.' He could hardly believe that wilful damage of such a masterpiece could have been 'accidental, or partly accidental, or contrary to the orders of a superior officer', and he added grimly: 'Should it turn out to be a predetermined destruction – as an object-lesson of the German ruling caste's will to power – it will strongly suggest that a disastrous blight upon the glory and nobility of that great nation has been wrought by the writings of Nietzsche, Treitschke, Bernhardi, &c.' When a number of correspondents wrote in to protest against what they conceived to be his misrepresentation of Nietzsche, he replied, on 13 October, that 'few men who have lived long enough to see the real colour of life, and who have suffered, can believe in Nietzsche as a thinker.' Hardy remembered the Germany of Kant and Schopenhauer, the older Germany whose cultural traditions had long been admired by men of England, and he found himself appalled by the 'curse of militarism' that had overtaken that land. When, only a few years after the Armistice, he was asked his opinion of a League of Thinkers (a proposal made by the son of Leo Tolstoy in an issue of *The New World*), he answered gloomily,

Though I have not as yet had time to consider closely the ways and means of promoting it, or how the Thinkers are to get themselves listened to by the Doers, think they never so wisely, I believe there are ways, and that it is only in those ways salvation lies, if there can be any salvation at all for a world that has got itself into such a deplorable welter, which seems to threaten a new Dark Age, to last may be for centuries before 'the golden years return.'

'A new Dark Age': this is the language of a dark and bitter mood. For Hardy's 'faith in the bettering of nations was shattered by the brutal unreason of the Continental instigators of the war' – such was his wording in a symposium printed in *The Times* on 29 December 1921 – and there is no evidence to show that it was ever made whole.

Thomas Hardy's life, it should be noted, covered most of the decades of *Pax Britannica*, but his faith in the continuing growth of common sense collapsed long before that moment in history when the British Empire covered the most land – 1921, the same year as the *Times* symposium. What I should like to do is define the nature of that faith; to look more closely at some of the poetry in which Hardy expressed his attitude toward war as a means of settling human grievances; and perhaps to arrive at some reasonable judgement on whether Hardy ever achieved a reconciliation of his love of England with his detestation of the nationalistic spirit. The undertaking is of some importance not only because Hardy's poetry was the place where he spoke most frankly of his deepest concerns (all his prose fictions were vulnerable to Grundyism, but he believed Mrs Grundy did not read poetry), but because any such consideration inevitably raises vast issues such as Hardy's concept of history and his understanding of his own 'philosophy' of 'evolutionary meliorism'.

Poems about war, as such, do not bulk large in Hardy's eight volumes of poems, or in the uncollected poems for which so much valuable information has been provided by J. O. Bailey in Part Two of his *Handbook*. Indeed, Hardy paid attention to only three wars in his poetry – the Napoleonic Wars between 1805 and 1815, the Boer War, and the Great War of 1914–18. But the longest poem he wrote, and the literary achievement of which he felt proudest, concerned itself entirely with war: *The Dynasts*, an enormous work of nineteen acts and 131 scenes, was far more than a reworking in a multitude of metres and rhyme-schemes of the historical period he had already treated in *The Trumpet-Major* and a number of short stories; it was his fullest development of the concept of Immanent Will, a full-length portrait of the Emperor Napoleon and partial portraits of more than one hundred other men and women, a conscious experiment with a controversial mixed form that he called 'epic-drama' (perhaps for want of a better name), and the end-product of more than a half-century of reading, interviews with survivors, and visits to battlefields. How he used his historical sources has been treated, with considerable sympathy and insight, by W. R. Rutland in *Thomas Hardy, a Study of his Writings and their Background* (1938), and all his sources, taken together, by Walter Wright in his enormously useful work, *The Shaping of 'The Dynasts'*. I need not review the trips that Hardy made to Chelsea Hospital, the British Museum, and Paris to get his facts right; yet it might be worth remarking that Hardy's famous footnote about the site of the Duchess of Richmond's ball in Brussels the night before Waterloo – 'The event happened less than a century ago, but the spot is almost as phantasmal in its elusive mystery as towered Camelot, the palace of Priam, or the hill of Calvary' (III.VI.ii) – is the final echo of a statement made by him in a letter to *The Times* (17 December 1888), that the Duchess of Richmond, during her stay in Brussels may have given more than one ball, 'or that at least, in addition to the last great ball, a small dance or two took place, and that one of these, magnified by a child's imagination, may have been the occasion. . . .'

Hardy's interest in the decade that had led up to the introduction of the true *Pax Britannica* (the years following Waterloo) amounted to an obsession, and it would be extraordinary if Hardy's detestation of war – a lifelong habit of mind – had not found expression in the descriptions of carnage-strewn battlefields from those of the Peninsular Campaign to those leading toward and away from Moscow. Those descriptions are so vivid, and our retrospective knowledge of how little they gained for Napoleon and all the other dynasts of Europe so secure, that a review of one such scene will suffice. Hardy has reproduced for us the full, grisly reality of Albuera, a battle that the English won after a 'ghastly climax':

> . . . the combatants are seen to be firing grape and canister at speaking distance, and discharging musketry in each other's faces when so close that their complexions may be recognized. Hot corpses, their mouths blackened by catridge-biting, and surrounded by cast-away knapsacks, firelocks, hats, stocks, flint-boxes, and priming-horns, together with red and blue rags of clothing, gaiters, epaulettes, limbs, and viscera, accumulate on the slopes, increasing from twos and threes to half-dozens, and from half-dozens to heaps, which steam with their own warmth as the spring rain falls gently upon them. (II.VI.iv)

Yet the final word is not given to one of Hardinge's fusiliers who carry the day; it is spoken by the Spirit of the Pities who, here as elsewhere, articulates Hardy's personal sense of anguish over the needless deaths of so many:

> Hide their hacked bones, Earth! – deep, deep, deep,
> Where harmless worms caress and creep. –
> What man can grieve? what woman weep?
> Better than waking is to sleep! Albuera!

Albuera, like all the battlefields, is where thousands of men may be seen 'wheeling'

> In moves dissociate from their souls' demand,
> For dynasts' ends that few even understand!

The notion that these lines verbalise is our helplessness to do other than what has been willed for us to do. The affinities between Hardy's Immanent Will and doctrines expounded by both Schopenhauer and Eduard Von Hartmann may often be coincidental, as F. B. Pinion has pointed out, but they are certainly striking. At any rate, Hardy did not claim to be original in his concept of the Immanent Will, and he often enough denied that he was employing it in his art as more than 'a plausible theory only'. Perhaps he never defended the historical antecedents of the Immanent Will more vigorously than in a letter he wrote to the *Times Literary Supplement* (19 February 1904), as part of a running argument with Arthur Bingham Walkley, the distinguished literary and dramatic critic:

> . . . The philosophy of *The Dynasts*, under various titles and phrases, is almost as old as civilization. Its fundamental principle, under the name of Predestination, was preached by St. Paul. "Being predestinated" – says the author of the Epistle to the Ephesians, "Being predestinated according to the purpose of Him who worketh all things after the counsel of His own Will"; and much more to the same effect, the only difference being that externality is assumed by the Apostle rather than immanence. It has run through the history of the Christian Church ever since. St. Augustine held it vaguely, Calvin held it fiercely, and, if our English Church and its Nonconformist contemporaries have now almost abandoned it to our men of science (among whom determinism is a commonplace), it was formerly taught by Evangelical divines of the finest character and conduct.

Albuera, in other words, had to happen as it did happen, and the lamentation of the Spirit of the Pities, too, is inevitable: 'I feel, Sire, as I must!' (I.I.vi). And at this point it may be appropriate to quote Hardy's contribution to a symposium in *The Young Man* (June 1901), written while he was working on *The Dynasts*: 'Aggressiveness being one of the laws of nature, by condemning war we condemn the scheme of the universe; while by exalting war we exalt sentiments which all worthy religions agree in calling evil, and whose triumphs the world would do well to escape by self-annihilation.'

Thomas Hardy hated war: so much seems clear. Napoleon was no more his own master than the soldiers he sent to do his bidding, and who all too often died for him; he was unable 'to shoulder Christ from out the topmost niche / In human fame', unable to 'assume the prophet or the demi-god, / A part past playing now', and unable to ensure that the King of Rome would succeed him upon the throne. In the wood of Bossu he brooded, with an insight that the Spirit of the Years commended as true,

> Great men are meteors that consume themselves
> To light the earth. This is my burnt-out hour.
>
> (III.VII.ix)

Still, there is something puzzling about Hardy's overall position on this matter of Napoleon's greatness, even though Napoleon is, in large measure, attempting to rationalise his defeat at Waterloo. How could Napoleon possibly have been a great man if the Immanent Will possesses the attributes that all the Spirits claim for it? Can *any* man be great in a universe ruled by the Immanent Will? Was it not the Spirit of the Years who referred to the human race in general as gyrating 'like animalcula / In tepid pools' (Fore Scene)? More puzzling still, why did Hardy, in his Preface, insist that an important motive in returning to the historical period treated by *The Trumpet-Major* was 'the slight regard paid to English influence and action throughout the struggle by so many Continental writers who had dealt with Napoleon's career', if he had not believed that English heroes – Pitt, Nelson, Wellington, those who had stopped Napoleon– deserved full recognition in a 'new handling of the theme which should re-embody the features of this influence in their true proportion'?

For what becomes evident, once we penetrate past the splendid imagery of the Immanent Will and the celestial machinery that Hardy reinvented for his modern fable, is that *The Dynasts* is, among other things, a celebration of the English will to resist tyranny. Badly led on occasion by politicians, a mad king, a Prince Regent unable to resist scandalous whims and relationships, England nevertheless emerges as a land congenial to heroes, at least three of whom are very large-scale. It is not only by their impassioned speeches on public occasions that their nobility may be measured (many of Wellington's most telling comments were laconic anyhow). Napoleon's anger at England's 'tough, enisled, self-centred, kindless craft' that finally destroyed him might be taken as authoritative testimony that England, more than any other nation, had undone him (from Hardy's point of view). All readers of *The Dynasts* know where Hardy's sympathies lay – with the dying Pitt, with 'dead Nelson and his half-dead crew', with the cool Wellington surveying one battlefield after another and swiftly, ingeniously exploiting his moments of opportunity. We are never in doubt that England's resistance to Boney was a good thing for both England and Europe. The Spirits are properly respectful to these giants of an earlier age. The Spirit of the Years applauds Pitt's great toast at the Guildhall as 'his last large words':

My lords and gentlemen: – You have toasted me
As one who has saved England and her cause.
I thank you, gentlemen, unfeignedly.
But – no man has saved England, let me say:
England has saved herself, by her exertions:
She will, I trust, save Europe by her example!

(I.V.V)

Nothing in the description of Trafalgar is touched by meanness, irony, or the mockings of the Spirit Sinister. And Wellington's victories sanguinary though they may be, are never belittled as having been pre-determined.

Heroism then became a concept of magnitude in Hardy's most extended statement on the horrors of war. Hardy could recognise its importance even on the French side, as – for example – when the Spirit of the Pities speaks of Ney as a 'hero of heroes' and a 'simple and single-souled lieutenant' (III.VII. iv). I will not attempt to trace, in my limited space, the full record of the scenes in which Hardy depicts the English nation persevering in its pursuit of a righteous cause – the destruction of an irresponsible tyrant. But he makes very clear that England, for many years, is conscious of the loneliness of its self-chosen role.

A work that undercuts the possibility of human greatness even as a few individuals, mostly English, are singled out for our attention as admirable and heroic: here, surely, is an irony the full implications of which have not been explored in Hardy criticism. And it is evident, too, that the comfortable feeling of the remoteness of war, fostered by the years of Pax Britannica, worked its fateful magic on even that most clear-sighted of men, Thomas Hardy.

How else are we to explain 'The Sick Battle-God', written in 1901, in which Hardy praised 'modern meditation', the humanitarian impulses of literature, and the obvious criminality of war as causes leading to the enfeeblement of the war-god in the twentieth century?

> . . . He rarely gladdens champions now:
> They do and dare, but tensely – pale of brow;
> And would they fain uplift the arm
> Of that weak form they know not how.
>
> Yet wars arise, though zest grows cold;
> Wherefore, at times, as if in ancient mould
> He looms, bepatched with paint and lath;
> But never hath he seemed the old!

> Let men rejoice, let men deplore,
> The lurid Deity of heretofore
> Succumbs to one of saner nod;
> The Battle-god is god no more.

The poet who could write those lines was capable of romanticising and idealising the past. 'The Bridge of Lodi' – which Hardy insisted, in a footnote, should be pronounced 'loddy' for the sake of his rhymes – marked the site of the victory against the Austrians that convinced Napoleon he was destined to conquer Europe: and yet none of the wives of Lodi knew anything about the relationship of the bridge to a notable moment in European history, because they were too busy with their 'transitory / Marketings in cheese and meat'. Hardy wondered, in that poem, whether war might be overrated, and whether his fascination with the site of an important battle had lost touch with the reality that 'the Lodi-bred ones' lived by late in the century. Perhaps the Lodi people were 'but viewing war aright'. Nevertheless, Hardy concluded – almost defiantly – by singing a song about 'The Bridge of Lodi', and describing it as that 'long-loved, romantic thing'.

From 'The Bridge of Lodi' it is but a small step to conjuring up the past as somehow better, more chivalric in its behaviour, than anything the modern world has to offer, even though Hardy knew well that thousands had died at Lodi, and that the consequence of the fight at the bridge had been Napoleon's new-found conviction that he was 'an exceptional man'. A notable statement to this effect, the poem 'Then and Now', was written in 1915 to contrast the murderousness of Herod (Germany) with the honour of 'the heroic schools' of the past. Hardy attacked the slaughter of civilians (as in Belgium) by positing an age when 'a chivalrous sense of Should and Ought' prevailed; when men faced one another 'in the open' as self-respecting knights; when

> They would not deign
> To profit by a stain
> On the honourable rules. . . .

Why did Hardy, on occasions, deceive himself about the honourableness of wars fought in the past? The answer is not easy to formulate. *The Dynasts* is certainly a devastating attack on the pretension that dynastic wars are in the interest of mankind. The best we can say is that Hardy was of more than one mind on the matter, and that his hopes for a future of international peace were directly related to the sense of security fostered by four generations of relative tranquillity. Hardy, in the *Later Years*, has told us that he disbelieved the 'music-hall Jingoes' who had been saying that 'Germany was as anxious for war as they were themselves', and that he had believed that 'common sense' had replaced 'bluster in men's minds'. Moreover, he based this conviction on 'a long study of the European wars of a century earlier', and he reminded his reader of a poem he had written as late as 1913, 'His Country', with its impassioned declaration of an international citizenship and its marginal gloss (an unusual accompaniment for any poem by Hardy), 'He travels southwards and looks around; / and cannot discover the boundary / of his native country; or where his duties to his fellow-creatures end; / nor who are his enemies.'

> I journeyed from my native spot
>   Across the south sea shine,
> And found that people in hall and cot
> Laboured and suffered each his lot
>   Even as I did mine. . . .

> I asked me: 'Whom have I to fight,
>   And whom have I to dare,
> And whom to weaken, crush, and blight?
> My country seems to have kept in sight
>   On my way everywhere.'

Hardy, I am suggesting, changed his mind on a matter of deep concern to his art. Is there, in fact, a significant difference between two groupings of his poems about the impact of war on the English people?

Let us begin with the eleven war poems, published in *Poems of the Past and the Present* as a set, that dealt with the Boer War. They include one poem we have already noted as unrealistic – Hardy himself might have called 'The Sick Battle-God' fatuous after the Great War imposed a heaviness upon his heart – but we must add that its cheerfulness was unrepresentative, and that Hardy for the most part was concerned with the meaning of the Boer War as perceived by its victims. As we might expect, the tone was compassionate: 'The Going of the Battery' bears as its subtitle 'Wives' Lament', and the poet thinks of the 'lists of killed and wounded' ('At the War Office, London') in terms of the grief caused to 'parent, wife, or daughter / By hourly posted sheets of scheduled slaughter.' One lyric is entitled 'Song of the Soldiers' Wives and Sweethearts', and though it exults in the return of the Household Cavalry 'no more, may be, to roam again', the poem breathes an atmosphere of regret that they ever had to go away.

Hardy's imagination is enlisted with 'The Souls of the Slain', with 'Drummer Hodge', and with the 'mouldering soldier' in South Africa whose 'puzzled phantom moans / Nightly to clear Canopus' about the justice of a war that has taken his life some twenty centuries after 'the All-Earth-gladdening Law / of Peace, brought in by that Man Crucified.' Even the Colonel who is departing for the war, and who soliloquises as his ship leaves behind the Southampton docks, knows that he is older now than when he journeyed on Her Majesty's service to 'Eastern lands and South'. He is not exultant, even though the word 'Hurrah!' turns up early in his musings; he is not given to cant; and Hardy, when he has concluded the series of poems which he called his 'war effusions', was justified in saying, with some pride, that 'not a single one is Jingo or Imperial.' Hardy doubtless shared his wife's view that the English cause was less clearly committed to the defence of 'homes & liberties' than that of the Boer soldiers. He was personally distressed that 'this late age of thought, and pact, and code' had failed to prevent the outbreak of the Boer War, and when he visited the scene of embarkation, he remembered Vespasian, Cerdic, and Henry V as having argued 'in the selfsame bloody mode' in earlier centuries. What the Boer War brought to England, in short, was the grief of civilians who lost their loved ones; the under-scoring of old and unworthy emotions about the glories of war (the sweethearts who 'prink' themselves 'in sables for heroes', for example); a vaguely disturbing sense of the tragedies played out under 'foreign constellations' and 'strange stars amid the gloam'. No man benefited from this war, nor woman either. Hardy's attitude, if one or two lines may express something as complex as the feelings that Hardy attuned and held in perilous balance, is to be found in the description of Drummer Hodge's funeral:

> They throw in Drummer Hodge, to rest
> Uncoffined – just as found. . . .

Hodge (as Hardy told us in both *Tess of the d'Urbervilles* and his long essay "The Dorsetshire Labourer") was the name given to a stereotype of a country bumpkin, who 'hangs his head or looks sheepish when spoken to, and thinks Lunnon a place paved with gold.' Who in England cares if such a 'pitiable picture known as Hodge' finds in South Africa an igno-minious funeral, without coffin, in a grave marked only by a 'kopje-crest That breaks the veldt around'? Drummer Hodge, for his pains, has earned only the meanest kind of death. The war has not won glory for the English at home, and for them the death of 'a supposed real but highly conventional Hodge' has, if anything, cheapened the possibility of a genuine emotional response. The idiosyncratic and personal identity of the real Hodge has been denied.

What were Hardy's poems about the Great War like? As we have seen, some testified to his willingness to respond to the English Cabinet's call for propagandistic literature: 'An Appeal to America on Behalf of the Belgian Destitute', 'A Call to National Service', and the song of the soldiers, 'Men Who March Away', are lyrics for the moment, war chants if you will, written by a poet in his late seventies who wished that he might be younger in order to 'serve with never a slack' a land that must not go 'untended as a wild of weeds and sand'. These are not wholly undistinguished poems – no lyric by Hardy lacks interest, or for that matter, biographical relevance – but they do not constitute a majority of the lyrics. For the most part his tone is angrier and grimmer than in his poems about the Boer War, and it darkened as the years of the Great War passed, and as more loved ones like his cousin, Second Lieutenant Frank William George of the Fifth Dorset Regiment, died as sacrificial victims.

An analysis of the reasons why Hardy could not write in bulk quantity the kind of poem that Chancellor Masterman had hoped for deserves a moment of our time. There was obviously the fact that he had never written much poetry to order, and would have been uneasy with the occasional poetry demanded in exchange for the perquisites of the Poet Laureateship. Beyond that, the battles of the Great War were astoundingly more bloody than most of the skirmishes of the Boer War, and the multitudinousness of the victims tended to numb the imaginative faculty that had produced his magnificent poem about the helpless animals at Waterloo in Part III of The Dynasts. (For example, Hardy was impressed by the fact that the Belgian destitute numbered 'seven millions'.) Still again, he was appalled by the tragedy of the German people warring against the English people ('kin folk kin tongued even as we are', he called the English and Germans in 'The Pity of It'), when all that both peoples wanted was to live in peace; the dynasts of an earlier age had turned into 'gangs whose glory threats and slaughters are', whose lust of power is 'insatiate', whose goal is 'but to swell and swell again / Their swollen All-Empery plans.' The peoples had been betrayed again. Hardy foresaw, even during the first months of war, that ancient friendships, shared experiences, a common love of learning, would be forgotten amidst the tumult and the shouting, as 'the wormwood-worded greeting' went up 'from each city, shore, and lea'. Somehow it all seemed so repetitive of earlier lunacies, so useless in what it sought to accomplish, so preordained. The first stanza of 'In Time of Wars and Tumults', written in 1915, is the lamentation of a man who regrets having lived long enough to see the outbreak of the Great War:

> 'Would that I'd not drawn breath here!' some one said,
> 'To stalk upon this stage of evil deeds,
> Where purposelessly month by month proceeds
> A play so sorely shaped and blood-bespread.'

But Hardy reassures us – he speaks *in propria persona* to make the point – that even if that 'some one' had never lived, 'Life would have swirled the same', that is to say, there would have been a Great War.

It is true that Hardy, in his often-quoted poem 'In Time of "The Breaking of Nations" ', written in 1915 at approximately the same period as 'In Time of Wars and Tumults', promises that some things – the harrowing of clods, the burning of couch-grass, the way of a man with a maid – 'will go onward the same / Though Dynasties pass.' Even so, what comfort was there in the passing of dynasties when, for each generation, the possibility of war remained? And not merely the possibility, but, as 1914 demonstrated, the reality of war on a scale that beggared even the dread anticipations of 'Channel Firing', a poem written three months before the German declaration of war against the Allied Powers; a poem in which God described the modern nations of Europe as 'mad as hatters', and noted that

> 'The world is as it used to be:
>
> 'All nations striving strong to make
> Red war yet redder. . . .'

This is the very real and most important difference between the poems written at the turn of the century and the poems of 1914 and 1915: whereas only a decade and a half earlier Hardy had identified as a means of ending war the growing sense of internationalism that produced, among many similar expressions of idealism, Norman Angell's phenomenally popular book, *The Great Illusion* (1910), Hardy had now become convinced that internationalism, however potent its promise, would not come to pass in his lifetime; and the realisation that it would not came close to breaking his heart. I do not speak hyperbolically. The evidence supports this reading of Hardy's mind.

Let us take a closer look at the gloom that settled down on Hardy in his final decade. It was far more than an inevitable effect of advancing age and a sense that any poems written now would be (as his posthumously published volume called them) *Winter Words*. He had lost the kind of assurance that Rudyard Kipling could sustain, despite the challenge to a civilised man's sense of reason posed by the Great War. In an essay called 'Winning the Victoria Cross', slightly revised for publication in *Land and Sea Tales* (1923), Kipling could still freely use words like 'honour' and 'glory', and could still write as his climactic sentence, '. . . for the real spirit of The Army changes very little through the years.' But something in Hardy's real spirit *had* changed.

'And There Was a Great Calm,' the poem that he wrote for the special Armistice Day section of *The Times* (printed 11 November 1920), was not, for example, a conventional rejoicing at the 'clemency' distilled from Heaven; he formulated no hopeful answer to the question of 'the bereft, and meek, and lowly', who asked whether men some day might be given to grace, whether indeed the hope of ancient dreams might come to pass. Propaganda, with the ugly words 'dug-outs', 'snipers', and 'Huns', had been multiplied by 'the war-adept' so effectively that 'the thinned peoples' could no longer hope. As Hardy wrote in his concluding stanza,

> Some could, some could not, shake off misery:
> The Sinister Spirit sneered: 'It had to be!'
> And again the Spirit of Pity whispered, 'Why?'

Hardy was resurrecting, in this post-war poem, the Spirits he had used with such sublime effect in *The Dynasts*, but something odd had happened: the Spirit of the Years, who customarily spoke for the deterministic point of view, had disappeared, and had been replaced by the sneering Spirit Sinister; nor did the poem indicate why or how the smirking of the Spirit of Irony was distinguishable, in any significant respect, from the sneering of the Spirit Sinister. J. O. Bailey, in the *Handbook*, comments shrewdly that 'Perhaps the pointless evil of World War I moved Hardy to let Sinister express the determinism of Years' point of view.' The poem – at any rate – does not attempt to answer the question of the Spirit of Pity, 'Why?' Hardy could not answer it for himself. As he wrote in the poem, 'Men had not paused to answer', and the philosophies of the sages, Selflessness and Loving-kindness had been too cruelly abused during the 'years of Passion'.

Hardy did not believe 'the Great Calm' of the Armistice was permanent. His final reading of the movement of history is contained in the sombre quatrain, 'Christmas: 1924' published posthumously in the *Daily Telegraph* three and a half years after that. I have referred to it already, but now quote it in its entirety:

> 'Peace upon earth!' was said. We sing it,
> And pay a million priests to bring it.

> After two thousand years of mass
> We've got as far as poison-gas.

Christianity had failed to keep the peace; it had deluded mankind; its promises could not be converted to reality.

Even as Hardy defended himself against the charges of disillusion and despair after the publication of *Time's Laughingstocks*, he spoke with some bitterness of the 'grinning optimism' of his contemporaries. Optimism of any kind was uncongenial to him in the 1920s; he did not believe in it. In his scattered statements on blood sports – which he detested – he wrote on the basis of the assumption that the human race was 'still practically barbarian' (as in his letter to *The Times*, printed on 5 March 1927). One of the mordant poems in *Late Lyrics and Earlier* (1922) comments on the clearing away of the wooden crosses from the old Western Front as material fit only for 'The Wood Fire' (a number of readers thought the poem blasphemous, and Edmund Blunden tells us that Hardy 'very keenly resented' the allegation). Hardy's views are clearly set forth in the 'Apology' prefixed to *Late Lyrics and Earlier*. Although this essay is well known because it redirects our attention to the second of Hardy's 'In Tenebris' poems, and to the line 'If way to the Better there be, it exacts a full look at the Worst', we ought to note how deeply ambiguous the line is; Hardy does not commit himself to the existence of 'the Better', and remarks only that the full look at the Worst necessarily comes first. More important to our concern with Hardy's cheerlessness during the 1920s, this is also the essay in which Hardy defines the differences between his kind of poetry and the poetry being written in 'neo-Georgian days'. He did not have much affection for what was then being called modern poetry; but he went further:

> The thoughts of any man of letters concerned to keep poetry
> alive cannot but run uncomfortably on the precarious prospects
> of English verse at the present day. Verily the hazards and
> casualties surrounding the birth and setting forth of almost every
> modern creation in numbers are ominously like those of one of
> Shelley's paper-boats on a windy lake. And a forward conjecture
> scarcely permits the hope of a better time, unless men's tendencies
> should change. So indeed of all art, literature, and 'high thinking'
> nowadays. Whether owing to the barbarizing of taste in the younger
> minds by the dark madness of the late war, the unabashed cultiva-
> tion of selfishness in all classes, the plethoric growth of knowledge
> simultaneously with the stunting of wisdom, 'a degrading thirst

after outrageous stimulation' (to quote Wordsworth again), or from any other cause, we seem threatened with a new Dark Age.

Now any number of observations might be made about Hardy's cast of mind as revealed by this passage, but the notion that men's minds appeared 'to be moving backwards rather than on' was repeated in several contexts, with barely any change in wording. In addition, whatever remedies he proposed – 'loving-kindness, operating through scientific knowledge, and actuated by the modicum of free will conjecturally possessed by organic life when the mighty necessitating forces – unconscious or other – that have "the balancing of the clouds" happen to be in equilibrium' – were not about to end this 'ominous moving backward'. What lay ahead? Knowledge of the future, if the future was in fact to be as bleak as Hardy suspected it would be, was not wanted by Hardy's compatriots. As he told Siegfried Sassoon, he did not believe that the League of Nations could prevent wars; whether wars came about from the operations of 'some demonic force' or from an innate love of violence really mattered little. In the ordering of his poems for *Winter Words*, he placed last the two most despairing declarations of a broken faith in evolutionary meliorism. The first of these poems was called 'We Are Getting to the End', but he was not talking simply about the end of his own life – by this time he was in his late eighties – but about the end of dreams as well:

> We are getting to the end of visioning
> The impossible within this universe,
> Such as that better while may follow worse,
> And that our race may mend by reasoning.

He no longer pretended that his view was guardedly hopeful. He was looking directly on the Worst, nor did he want to share with others what he knew, what he might discern or suspect about the future.

The second of his two final poems is called 'He Resolves to Say No More', and it implies strongly that Hardy foresaw the certainty of the Second World War, and of wars beyond that:

> O my soul, keep the rest unknown!
> It is too like a sound of moan
> When the charnel-eyed
> Pale Horse has nighed:
> Yea, none shall gather what I hide!

Hardy, whose knowledge of the Testaments was as keen as that of any poet of the last century, must have had in mind Revelation 6:8: 'And I looked, and beheld a pale horse: and his name that sat on him was Death, and Hell followed with him.' At the end of his life, he would promise no man to show what he saw, and not simply because he foresaw the approach of the pale horse to himself as an individual, but because he had compassion for his fellow-man:

> Why load men's minds with more to bear
> That bear already ails to spare?

None of the writers gathered around that table in Wellington House on 3 September 1914 could foresee, as Hardy wrote, 'in all their completeness the tremendous events that were to follow.' Nor, in the final irony of his noble, distinguished, and productive life, could Hardy, himself a participant in that historic moment, foresee that he himself would finally renounce his faith in the powers of reason, science, and the evolving consciousness of the Immanent Will to create a better world.

Notes

INTRODUCTION

1. This page is reproduced as a photograph in Richard Little Purdy's
   Thomas Hardy, A Bibliographical Study (London and New York: Oxford
   University Press, 1954) after p. 272.
2. Helmut E. Gerber and W. Eugene Davis, *Thomas Hardy: An Annotated
   Secondary Bibliography of Writings About Him* (De Kalb, Ill.: Northern
   Illinois University Press, 1973) p. 11.
3. *The Life of Thomas Hardy 1840–1928* by Florence Emily Hardy (1933; repr.
   London: Macmillan, 1962; New York: St Martin's Press, 1962) p. 284.
4. Carl J. Weber, *Hardy's Love Poems* (London: Macmillan, 1962; New
   York: St. Martin's Press, 1962) pp. v–vii.

CHAPTER 1

1. This is Paul Zietlow's argument, developed with considerable elo-
   quence, in *Moments of Vision: The Poetry of Thomas Hardy* (Cambridge,
   Mass.: Harvard University Press, 1974) pp. 246–7.
2. John Cowper Powys, *The Pleasures of Literature* (London: Cassell, 1938)
   pp. 612–13.
3. *Life*, pp. 214–15.
4. *Thomas Hardy's Notebooks and Some Letters from Julia Augusta Martin*, edited by
   Evelyn Hardy (London: Hogarth Press, 1955) pp. 127–8.
5. *Life*, p. 18
6. *Life*, p. 87.
7. *Life*, p. 50.
8. *Life*, p. 48.
9. *Some Recollections by Emma Hardy*, edited by Evelyn Hardy and Robert
   Gittings (London: Oxford University Press, 1961; Freeport, New
   York: Books for Libraries, 1972) p. 12.
10. Weber, *Hardy's Love Poems*, p. 39.
11. F. B. Pinion, *A Hardy Companion* (London: Macmillan, 1968; New York:
    St. Martin's Press, 1968) p. 29.
12. Frank Ernest Halliday, *Thomas Hardy: His Life and Work* (Bath, Somerset:
    Adams & Dart, 1972; New York: Barnes & Noble, 1972) p. 110.

13. Carl J. Weber and Clara Carter Weber, *Thomas Hardy's Correspondence at Max Gate: A Descriptive Check List* (Waterville, Maine: Colby College Press, 1968) pp. 14–15.

14. *One Rare Fair Woman: Thomas Hardy's Letters to Florence Henniker 1893–1922* edited by Evelyn Hardy and F. B. Pinion (London: Macmillan, 1972; Coral Gables: University of Miami Press, 1972) pp. xxiii–xxiv. The quoted statements occur in the first preface, written by Evelyn Hardy.

15. *'Dearest Emmie': Thomas Hardy's Letters to his First Wife*, edited by Carl J. Weber (London: Macmillan, 1963; New York: St. Martin's Press, 1963) pp. 101–2.

16. *The Shop Assistant* (21 June 1919) p. 405.

17. R. J. White, in *Thomas Hardy and History* (London: Macmillan, 1974; New York: Barnes & Noble, 1974), characterises Hardy as typically Victorian in his tastes for the writers of historical studies, and adds that Hardy 'belonged to a time and place which regarded everything in its historical bearings and thought everything was to be understood in historical items. Not only understood but explained. If one wanted to know why things were what they were, and not otherwise, one found out their history. History was not only explanation but justification' (p. 131).

18. Hardy argued that a marriage 'should be dissolvable at the wish of either party, if that party prove it to be a cruelty to him or her, provided (probably) that the maintenance of the children, if any, should be borne by the bread-winner,' This contribution to a symposium, 'How Shall We Solve the Divorce Problem?', was printed in *Nash's Magazine* (March 1912) p. 683, and continued a line of thought familiar to readers of *Jude the Obscure*.

19. Hardy 'did not know why animals were here – he told me once that he did not know why anything was born. That life to Man or beast was part of the divine purpose he was aware. But the suffering flung to the innocent was beyond his comprehension. All animals – however insignificant – seemed to him to have some mysterious mission. A hedgehog, he once remarked, is a piece of Divine creation which God, for some reason of His own, has put under spikes.' (Newman Flower, *Just as It Happened* (London: Cassell, 1950) p. 93.) The topic is treated more fully in Chapter 5 of the present book.

20. *Just as It Happened*, p. 100.

21. William Archer, *Real Conversations* (London: Heinemann, 1904) p. 45.

22. *Life*, p. 17. Some of my interpretations and emphases in this chapter differ from those of Robert Gittings's *Young Thomas Hardy* (London:

Heinemann, 1975), a brilliant examination of all the evidence lying behind Hardy's ingeniously distorted *Life*. Readers interested in learning more about the man behind the books dealing with Wessex will find Gittings a sympathetic and trustworthy biographer. I agree with Gittings that 'The true story of Hardy's early life is . . . essential to the understanding of some of his finest work' (p. 6).

CHAPTER 2

1. Carl J. Weber, *Hardy of Wessex, His Life and Literary Career* (1940; repr. Hamden, Conn.: Archon Books, 1962; London: Routledge, 1965) p. 170.

2. Quoted by J. O. Bailey, *The Poetry of Thomas Hardy: A Handbook and Commentary* (Chapel Hill and London: University of North Carolina Press, 1970) p. 24.

3. Clive Holland, *Thomas Hardy, O. M., The Man, His Works, and the Land of Wessex* (London: Herbert Jenkins, 1933) p. 179.

4. *Thomas Hardy's Personal Writings*, ed. Harold Orel (Lawrence: University of Kansas Press, 1966; London: Macmillan, 1967) p. 119.

5. *Concerning Thomas Hardy*, ed. D. F. Barber (London: Charles Skilton, 1968) pp. 76–7.

6. Bailey, *The Poetry of Thomas Hardy*, p. 388.

7. The frequency of his visits to Horace Moule, who diligently encouraged him to continue writing after the appearance of a number of adverse reviews, and who shared so many interests with him, decreased strikingly during this same period; the two men were, after all, living in different cities. Moule's suicide on 21 September 1873 ended a fifteen-year friendship that had, for several reasons, meant a great deal to Hardy. Hardy never had the opportunity to introduce Emma to his best friend, and he speculated, on more than one occasion, how the two might have gotten along with each other.

8. The statistics of distribution might, for the moment, be worth reviewing (they are taken from Carl Weber's *Hardy's Love Poems*, p. 102): poems about Emma were published in each of Hardy's collections of poems –two in *Wessex Poems*, three in *Poems of the Past and the Present*, three in *Time's Laughingstocks*, and then, beginning with the volumes of greatest interest to us, 32 in *Satires of Circumstance, Lyrics, and Reveries*, 33 in *Moments of Vision*, 25 in *Late Lyrics and Earlier*, 16 in *Human Shows, Far Phantasies*, and two in *Winter Words*, making a total of 116 poems.

9. F. B. Pinion, *A Hardy Companion*, pp. 351–3.

10. Hardy, in 'The Wind's Prophecy', may be recording the way in which

his romantic attachment to Tryphena declined, but the meagreness
of particularised statement here, as elsewhere, inhibits speculation.
11. Purdy, *Thomas Hardy: A Bibliographical Study*, p. 201.

CHAPTER 3

1. John Malcolm Brinnin, *The Sway of the Grand Saloon: A Social History of the North Atlantic* (New York: Delacorte Press, 1971) p. 382.
2. *One Rare Fair Woman*, p. 185.
3. Merryn Williams, *Thomas Hardy and Rural England* (London: Macmillan, 1972; New York: Columbia University Press, 1972) p. 154.
4. Donald Davie, *Thomas Hardy and British Poetry* (New York: Oxford University Press, 1972; London: Routledge, 1973) p. 38.
5. *Life*, p. 352.
6. *The Mayor of Casterbridge*, Chapter 11.
7. *Thomas Hardy's Personal Writings*, pp. 191–5.
8. *Life*, p. 14.
9. *Life*, p. 251.
10. *Life*, p. 296.
11. *Personal Writings*, pp. 197–8.
12. *Life*, p. 296.
13. *Life*, p. 436.
14. *Life*, p. 418.
15. *Life*, p. 282.
16. *Life*, p. 403.
17. *Life*, p. 337.
18. *Life*, p. 308.
19. *Life*, p. 306.
20. *Life*, pp. 405–6.
21. *Life*, p. 347.
22. *Life*, p. 349.
23. *Life*, p. 405.
24. *Life*, p. 370.
25. *Life*, p. 428.
26. *Life*, p. 419. Cf. pp. 347 and 385.
27. *Life*, p. 317.
28. *Life*, p. 328.
29. *Concerning Thomas Hardy*, p. 102.
30. *Life*, p. 389.
31. *Life*, p. 363.
32. W. M. Parker, 'A Visit to Thomas Hardy', *Monographs on the Life, Times*

and Works of Thomas Hardy, No. 24 (Beaminster, Dorset: Toucan Press, 1966) pp. 5–6.

33. Vere H. Collins, *Talks with Thomas Hardy at Max Gate: 1920–1922* (London: Duckworth, 1928) p. 49.

34. *Life*, p. 402.

35. *Thomas Hardy's Notebooks and Some Letters from Julia Augusta Martin*, ed. Evelyn Hardy (London: Hogarth Press, 1955) p. 113.

36. *Life*, p. 386.

37. *Life*, pp. 312–13.

38. See, in Williams, *Thomas Hardy and Rural England*, the Appendix, 'Population Movements in Some Dorsetshire Parishes 1840–1900', pp. 200–5.

39. 'Apology', *Personal Writings*, pp. 51–2; cf. pp. 54–5.

CHAPTER 4

1. *Life*, p. 28.

2. Introduction, *Jude the Obscure* (Indianapolis and New York: Bobbs-Merrill Co., Inc., 1972) p. xviii.

3. 1940; reprinted 1962 with a list of addenda and corrigenda, and revised for a new edition in 1965.

4. See Chapter One, 'Impressions of Reality', in Walter Wright's *The Shaping of 'The Dynasts'* (Lincoln: University of Nebraska Press, 1967) pp. 1–55, for an especially careful treatment of the literary debts incurred by Hardy in the composition of his epic-drama.

5. Page 84.

6. *Life*, p. 417.

7. *Life*, p. 402.

8. *Thomas Hardy's Notebooks*, p. 113.

9. *Concerning Thomas Hardy*, p. 102.

10. *Thomas Hardy's Personal Writings*, p. 145.

11. Vere H. Collins, in *Talks with Thomas Hardy*, records Hardy's observation about the writer Hudson, 'It must have been very sad for him to outlive all his friends' (p. 70).

12. 'Apology', Preface to *Late Lyrics and Earlier*, reprinted in *Thomas Hardy's Personal Writings*, p. 52.

13. *Life*, p. 443.

14. *Life*, p. 404.

15. *Life*, p. 388.

16. *Thomas Hardy's Personal Writings*, pp. 49–50.

17. *Life*, p. 378.

CHAPTER 5

1. *Life*, pp. 314–15.
2. Frank R. Southerington. *Hardy's Vision of Man* (London: Chatto and Windus, 1971; New York: Barnes & Noble, 1971) p. 69.
3. *Notes on 'The Dynasts', in Four Letters to Edward Clodd* (Edinburgh: Dunedin Press, 1929) pp. 10–11.
4. *Life*, p. 173.
5. *Concerning Thomas Hardy*, pp. 115–16.
6. Collins, *Talks with Thomas Hardy*, pp. 36–7.
7. *One Rare Fair Woman*, p. 174.
8. *Concerning Thomas Hardy*, p. 131.
9. *Life*, p. 400.
10. *Life*, p. 421.
11. *Life*, p. 431.
12. *Life*, p. 437.
13. *Concerning Thomas Hardy*, p. 117.
14. *Concerning Thomas Hardy*, p. 115.
15. The letter, dated 18 December, was printed on 19 December.
16. *Life*, p. 303.
17. *Life*, pp. 321–2.
18. *Life*, pp. 346–7.

CHAPTER 6

1. *Friends of a Lifetime: Letters to Sydney Carlyle Cockerell* (London: Jonathan Cape, 1940) p. 284.
2. Weber, *Hardy of Wessex*, pp. 90–1.
3. *Life*, p. 411. For additional comments by Hardy on the picturesqueness of the mummers, who were active in Dorset 'till 1880, or thereabouts', see Archer's *Real Conversations*, pp. 33–6. The visitors of 1920 were self-consciously reviving the tradition after years of neglect.
4. Ibid., p. 423.
5. Bailey, *The Poetry of Thomas Hardy*, p. 653.
6. Reginald Snell, 'A Self-Plagiarism by Thomas Hardy', *Essays in Criticism*, II (January 1952), pp. 114–17.

CHAPTER 7

1. *Life*, p. 285.
2. *Life*, p. 392.

3. At the final moments Hardy wished read to him 'The Listeners', by Walter de la Mare; 'Rabbi Ben Ezra', by Robert Browning; and a single verse from FitzGerald's translation of the *Rubáiyát of Omar Khayyám*. Hardy, unlike the dying Keats, was not feverishly attempting to rediscover the validity of Christian perspectives. Keats, as readers will recall, requested that Severn bring him a number of religious works, including Jeremy Taylor's *Holy Living and Holy Dying*, but none of these reassured him.

4. *Thomas Hardy's Personal Writings*, p. 57.

5. *Life*, p. 376.

6. Kenneth Phelps, *Annotations by Thomas Hardy in his Bibles and Prayer-Book* (St Peter Port, Guernsey: Toucan Press, 1966) *passim*.

7. Bailey, *The Poetry of Thomas Hardy*, p. 592.

8. Not much weight should be placed on the sequence of poems in *Winter Words*. As Florence Hardy wrote to Macmillan (11 February 1928), while the manuscript was being typed, 'The first poems and the last few have been arranged but I am not sure that the ones in the middle of the book were arranged. No doubt there would have been considerable revision.' (Hardy had died on 11 January.) 'A Nightmare, and the Next Thing' is one of the unarranged poems.

9. *Thomas Hardy's Notebooks*, p. 95.

10. *Life*, pp. 332–3.

11. Collins, *Talks with Thomas Hardy*, p. 63.

12. *The Letters of Thomas Hardy*, ed. Carl J. Weber (Waterville, Maine: Colby College Press, 1954) p. 100.

Index